Memoir of
the Bookie's Son

To Carol Werton with
gratitude for sharing
your wisdom with my
granddaughters. Cheers, too,
for your million dollar
smile!!

S. dy Offit

8 March 2000

Memoir of the Bookie's Son

Sidney Offit

St. Martin's Griffin
New York

A THOMAS DUNNE BOOK FOR ST. MARTIN'S GRIFFIN.
An imprint of St. Martin's Press.

A version of Chapter 1 appeared in *Confrontation* © 1992
by Long Island University

Design by Ellen R. Sasahara

LIBRARY OF CONGRESS CATALOGING-IN-PUBLICATION DATA

Offit, Sidney.
    Memoir of the bookie's son/Sidney Offit.
        p.   cm.
    "A Thomas Dunne book" for St. Martin's Griffin
    ISBN 0-312-14368-0 (hardcover)
    1. Offit, Sidney—Childhood and youth.   2. Bookmakers
(Gambling)—Maryland—Baltimore—Biography.   3. Fathers
and sons—Maryland—Baltimore—Biography.   4. Authors,
American—20th century—Biography.   5. Baltimore (Md.)—
Social life and customs.   I. Title.
PS3565.F385Z47   1995
813'.54—dc20
[B]   95–1759
                                                              CIP

First St. Martin's Griffin Edition: June 1996

·10   9   8   7   6   5   4   3   2   1

To my dad and mom's home team—Avi,
Benson, and Suzanne, Ken and Emily,
Mike and Dara, Andy and Suzie, Meg,
Tommy, Anna, Caroline, Tristan, Wyatt,
Lily, Adam, and David.

———————◆———————

CONTENTS

Spring—1992

Several days before the running of the Belmont, I spoke to my father on the telephone. I called from New York. Since my mother's death the previous spring, he had been living with my brother and sister-in-law in Baltimore. Toward the end of our brief conversation, I asked my dad the ritual question I learned as a child from his colleagues, family, and strangers: "What's your best bet for the day, Buckley?"

My father and mother were born and raised in Baltimore. Both their families had emigrated from a small Russian town in the last decades of the nineteenth century. My father was named Barney, but he was known as Buckley or Buck.

*   *   *

———————◆———————

After he returned from naval service in World War I, until the fifties when the Kefauver Committee recommended a federal stamp to identify professional gamblers, my dad and his partner Willis Buzz King had been among the elite of the nation's bookmakers. The owners, the trainers, and the high-stakes horse players relied upon them for bets that insiders didn't want influencing the odds at the track. These clients were a source of information and, from time to time, my dad remarked he "rode with the smart money." At the age of ninety-five, he had outlived the improvers of the breed who provided tips as well as business, so I was surprised that afternoon when he responded to my request for a handicapper's choice and told me, "The price is right, bet Strike the Gold."

Discussions of sports and politics were our catechism, though he neither encouraged nor seemed to expect me to follow through on opinions. Yet there was something about the gravity of his voice after so many long silences that made me believe this bet was important to him. Several weeks ear-

lier my father—with his gravel voice and diction so indigenous to Baltimore that the chamber of commerce provided a translation for English-speaking visitors—had told me, "What that kid brother of yours doin' for me ain't in the book. And that wife of hisn—Suzie—I wisht I had a package for 'em, so they ain't stuck with my tab."

My father didn't have pipe dreams. I wondered if his mind was slipping or rising to mystic heights. He could read only with great effort and depended upon television for news. How had he learned about Strike the Gold? The name conjured images of the last buck bet on a horse that wins and delivers the mother lode. But it seemed unlikely that my dad would ever subscribe to a sentimental hunch. The day before the Belmont I dropped by the OTB parlor on Second Avenue and Seventieth Street to check the line.

The sidewalk in front of the betting shop looked like an assembly of the homeless. Men in stained shirts, old baseball caps (one green and white number a souvenir of Las Vegas), and various fits of jeans collected in small clusters or stood

*alone studying the form on the 3" × 7" tickets
where they'd indicate their bets. There wasn't a tie
or suit jacket in the crowd—no style or expression
with which I could link the OTB customers on
the east side of Manhattan with the warm memories I had of my father's cronies in Baltimore fifty
years ago.*

*I went directly to the board displaying the day's
races. The roster seemed to be written in code. It
required several minutes for me to realize* HIA YON
FNG SPL PIM *wasn't the name of a Chinese restaurant but abbreviations for the names of tracks. I
searched the list of horses entered for the Belmont
Stakes*—Pine Bluff, Casual Lies, Agincourt,
My Memories, A.P. Indy. *There was no mention of* Strike the Gold *in the eighth race. I was
pleased to have an excuse to chuck my card*—
NEW YORK CITY OTB—EXOTIC BETS—BET WITH
YOUR HEAD, NOT OVER IT—. *I had a momentary
impulse to talk to one of the bettors and ask about*
Strike the Gold, *but I chalked it up to an old
man's vagrant memory, and took off for the weekend without further thought about the triple
crown race and long shots.*

Leafing through the sports pages of Newsday

for the late baseball scores the following Sunday, I read, "Strike the Gold rallies in Nassau . . .

For six races speed was the king yesterday at Belmont Park. If you weren't on or near the early lead on the muddy, slippery surface you were finished, regardless of how fast the fractions were. *Strike the Gold,* the *Silky Sullivan* of his generation was running in the seventh race, the 1 1/8th mile Nassau County Handicap . . .

The report went on to say that the 1991 Kentucky Derby Winner paid $11.60 for a $2 win ticket. "The price is right," my father had told me, "bet Strike the Gold." I was so pleased my old man hadn't lost his touch that I didn't begin to think until later that once again I'd let him down.

CHAPTER I

Take Me,
Take Me Dead

◆ *Baltimore, Maryland* ◆
Spring 1934

I am waiting for my father. It is 5:30. The mellifluous voice from the Philco announces, "Terry and the Pi-rates." From behind the furls of drapes in the front room of our house, I see a dark sedan stationed on the street directly in front of the entrance to our building. Across the island of green that traverses the avenue, the familiar figure in the double-breasted suit and grey hat approaches. My heart leaps in expectation of the gruff voice and reassuring greeting, "What d'ya say, Sid? Hit any long shots today?"

My father walks with the rolling gait of an athlete. His hands hang loosely at his sides as if prepared to catch a ball or curl quickly to throw a punch. He is passing the hedges and aluminum garbage cans when two men rush from the sedan. The more imposing of them is much taller than my father. He wears a long overcoat that reaches to his ankles, and a broad-brimmed hat. As he approaches my father, I see that he's wearing gloves. His partner seems dressed for another season. He has no coat. The sleeves of his shirt are rolled up. His black hair is slicked back and shiny. One of his pockets bulges.

They approach my father. I can't hear what they're saying but I see my father shake his head no. The tall man raises his hands, but before he touches my father a sudden, swift fist to the jaw knocks him off balance.

My father pivots and brings his other hand around, connecting with the smaller man. The man in the overcoat locks his arms around my father's neck. They struggle and trip. From the sidewalk I hear my father's voice: "I ain't going noplace with nobody." The man in shirtsleeves takes the gun from his pocket and jabs it at my father's ribs.

My eyes fill with tears. I am unable to make any sound other than a whimper.

As they struggle on the sidewalk a third man emerges from the car. He stands with one foot on the running board and shouts directions. "Get that bastard moving. Now." The figures blur but I am aware of my father kicking and swinging and finally coming up with the lid to the garbage can. There is the metallic sound of the aluminum can rolling on the pavement and my father's voice, "You take me, you take me dead." They try to pull my father into their car, but he kicks and twists and breaks away from their grasp.

Later my father returns home with his head swaddled in bandages and dark bruises under his eyes. His left arm is in a sling and he limps slightly. From the kitchen I see police officers sitting with our parents. I hear my father say, "That's right, gentlemen, I take bets. That's the way I make my living. But I never seen them punks before, and I got no idea who would've done a thing like that to me."

My father never talked about his injuries. He

stayed home for several days, working from the family telephone. The calls were brief. Standing by the phone, my father would repeat names and numbers and scratch the information on small slips of note paper. It was the only period of our childhood that I recall my father at home when I came back from school at midday. He always greeted us with a smile and a hug and the same question: "How'd it go at yer office today?" So as not to disturb him, our mother shuffled us into our room or out to play on the small porch that overlooked the back alley. When he took calls or sat at the dining room table to do his tabulations (which he referred to as "figuring up") he never expressed annoyance or seemed inhibited by our presence.

My parents didn't discuss the attempted kidnapping. It was such a startling moment of violence in what I considered a peaceful childhood that for years I erased it from my memory. Violence seemed so inconsistent with my father's behavior at home; it was difficult to identify the gentle hands that stroked our foreheads before we went to bed at night, or lightly frogged our arms to express approval, as the same ones that flailed at enemies so precisely and with such ease.

My father never hit me and only once went after my brother. Benson couldn't have been more than two years old when he woke my dad from a deep sleep on the couch by tapping him on the head with a miniature baseball bat. I recall my father rising in a fury and chasing my brother down the hall. But Benson reached my mother's arms. After a cautionary speech from her, my dad calmed down. Still, I remembered the expression of anger and the suggestion that the quiet, warm man who spoke from the corners of his mouth with the diction of the underworld was capable of physical rage.

CHAPTER II

Shoeboxes of Fifties

I was twelve years old the year we moved from a two-bedroom apartment overlooking an island of park in midtown Baltimore to a flat that included a study and second bathroom and was situated in the shadow of the Druid Reservoir.

My brother and I shared a bedroom and were offered the option of rooms of our own. It may have been the pretense of a "library" that inspired my ambitions for the third bedroom, but I was unwilling to give up my brother Benson's company. My mother installed bookcases along with a desk and sofabed in the back room. My collection of Big Little Books, mustered side by side with Louis Untermeyer's *Singing World*, the early volumes of Will Durant's *Story of Phi-*

losophy and the collected works of Arthur Conan Doyle. To go from the kitchen table to a desk and bookshelves would, I was certain, encourage me to study and "apply myself" to homework.

The move seemed to be undertaken for the benefit of my brother and me. My father never complained about our former quarters and seemed content to conduct his business from a phone in the hall and a seat at the dining room table.

The previous tenant of the apartment on Lake Drive to which we moved was a Mr. Sagner. I understood he was a clothing manufacturer and was delighted several months after we moved to discover he was the owner of a racehorse, *Saggy,* a three-year-old contender for some of racing's richest prizes. Although it was just a coincidence, I regarded living at the Sagner's former apartment as a legacy from one racing buff to another.

Until my twelfth year I had never thought seriously about money. My father didn't carry a wallet. A roll of bills was always available from either of his trouser pockets: a thick roll of ones and fives which he withdrew from his right and a more modest assembly of higher denominations deposited in the left. He transferred the rolls when he changed suits. Bills were never displayed on night tables. On one occasion when I popped into my parents' bed early in the morning, I remember encountering a particularly thick roll of money under the pillow on my father's side of the double bed.

I may have been five years old when I found this small treasure. My father always slept soundly. When he awoke he immediately proceeded about his business. Unlike my father, my mother seemed always to be awake. She would respond to my faintest whisper at night, and on Sunday mornings when I woke my brother to join me on the expedition to our parents' bed, my mother greeted us with open arms. I enjoyed snuggling between my parents. The contrast between my mother's soft, fleshy warmth and my father's muscular body and grizzled face amused and delighted me. Although he had no patience for the bed-play, my father didn't seem critical of it. As soon as he was up he would give us both a hug and start toward the bathroom, coffee, and morning paper.

The morning I discovered the money under his pillow—could it have been more than one roll?—I was as fascinated by the thick rubber bands as the booty they contained. My mother was distracted with Benson and my dad still asleep when I started unwrapping the money. The bills cascaded over my father's face and chest. He swatted them, opened his eyes, and looked at me with familiar affection before reacting. It was one of the rare times I remember my father ever expressing any confusion about his perception. "What the hell's going on here?" he said.

Bills were strewn across the pillow and had fallen onto the floor. My mother was less alarmed. "It's an accident, Buck. An accident."

My father collected several of the bills and examined them. "Jesus—my bankroll. How'd Sid get a hold of my bankroll?"

I was delighted. My brother joined me in the game, scrambling for the loose bills. My father's mood shifted abruptly. "Gimme that." He removed the small stack of bills which remained in my hands and retrieved the notes that were spread like confetti over the bedding and floor. When I tried to help him, he shooed me away. After he reassembled the bills, he counted them and wrapped them in several smaller bundles held by the rubber bands I had left on the night table. "How'd you get a hold of my package?" he asked with more curiosity than anger.

My mother answered for me, "It was under your pillow, Buck. You were sleeping . . . "

My father required no further explanation. He deposited the rolls of bills into the pockets of his trousers, which he always hung neatly over a chair before retiring for the night. "Don't ever mess with my money," he said, jabbing a finger in my direction. "If you want money, just ask for it."

"That's not the point, Buck," my mother said. "Sidney didn't want your money. He just found it by accident and was playing with it."

My father started to the bathroom. "Don't play with my money," he concluded gently. "You get a little older, you'll realize how much hustle goes into a package like that."

Later that Sunday after we had completed our ritual visit to my father's sister Aunt Ida, my father parked the Buick in front of a general store on Reisterstown Road. While he picked up two packages of Herbert Tarrytons, Benson and I window-shopped the collection of bronze soldiers in the showcase.

"Whaddya want, kids?" said my dad. It was the signal for his generosity. I knew he would buy us anything we wanted. I felt a vague embarrassment about this indulgence or, perhaps, even the suspicion that it was a test. I always limited my selections to a single book or one soldier or no more than three-for-a-dime candy bars. That morning I pretended not to want anything. Benson selected a helmeted doughboy carrying a tommy gun. "Sure you don't want nothing, Sid?"

When I shook my head no, my father instructed the merchant to give me a soldier with a tommy gun and "a couple of them guys on horses." We were on our way to the car when he said, "We gotta protect our bankroll to keep you boys in toys and hotcakes."

Although I frequently returned to my parents' bed for the Sunday hugs after that, I never found another roll of bills under the pillow.

Soon after we moved to Lake Drive, my mother instructed the building's janitor to remove the wooden frame that extended from the ceiling to the shower of the small bathroom adjoining our parents' bedroom. My father, who seemed indifferent to furnishings and decor, was unusually interested in the project. He stood on the kitchen ladder and examined the space; when a carpenter replaced the boards he tested that they were easily removable and repainted them to blend with the woodwork. Several days after the job was completed, my mother assembled a dozen shoeboxes. I noticed that the Keds and overshoes, which had previously been stored neatly in their original boxes from Hess Shoes, were now lined up at the rear of the closet floor.

Late one evening my father sat at the dining room table. Stuffed paper bags lay in front of him. One by one he emptied their contents — stacks and rolls of money. I had never seen such a mass of bills assembled in such volume. Compared to my father's fortune, the green and yellow and purple bills of the Monopoly game seemed scaled for purchases in a candy store. My father, indifferent to our fascinated attention, counted and stacked the piles of hundreds and fifties before my mother stored them neatly in the empty shoeboxes. We were still awake when my father banked his fortune in the hollow space above the bathroom shower. "There's our bankroll, kids," he said. "Say nothin' to nobody."

CHAPTER III

Play Action

The language of my father's work was familiar to me at an early age. Soon after I mastered the vocabulary—Mommy, Daddy, Gimme, Thank-you—I mimicked the words I heard my father say in the evening when he responded to the last bets of the day over our hall telephone. I later learned he would be receiving bets from the tracks that closed late—Santa Anita on the West Coast and Tijuana in Mexico.

When my father knew he would be using the phone, he would say to my mother, "I got action, honey, so don't tie up the line." The word "action" became synonymous with his occupation and, because the term "parlay the winner" was the most frequent of his terse responses, I determined that this was what the action was about. Other routine conversations included monosyllabic signals from my father to the person on the other end of the line: "Favorite . . . Scratch . . . Long shot . . . Eight to five . . . " plus a series of proper nouns, which I later learned identified tracks, horses, and players.

I remember volunteering my fragmented intelligence to my mother's mother, my beloved Bubby, who unlike my parents seemed to encourage my ambition to "work like my father." I wasn't quite five years old when I collected scraps of my father's slips from the garbage and saved them for Bubby so she could place pretend bets with me and we could play "action." I imitated my father's routine with the slips. When my mother discovered this charade she spoke spiritedly to Bubby in Yiddish. I cried when the shreds of slips were destroyed—not from anger but from disappointment.

My mother explained to me gently but firmly that I was never to play with any of the papers related to my father's work. She made it clear to me, too, that I should not discuss my father's business with other people. It was best that

Bubby and I amuse ourselves with make-believe entertainments and less authentic props.

I felt a curtain had been lowered that separated our family from the rest of the world. My father said nothing to me about the incident with Bubby but he never left a shred of a slip in a wastebasket after that. He didn't trust the building's incinerator, either. Although we had a chute in our apartment, my father tore the slips into small pieces and flushed them down the toilet.

Years passed before I understood the nature of my father's work. Because members of the family, neighbors, and the men we encountered at Oriole Park deferred to him, I was certain my father's vocabulary and the slips were related to an activity of worldly importance. The secrecy strengthened our family ties and though there seemed to be an undefined risk about my father's activities, I was certain he was strong enough, brave enough, and wise enough to overcome all challenges and protect us, too.

From time to time when a friend would ask, "What does your father do?" I would answer, "Parlay the winner." This term was as enigmatic to other six-year-olds as it was to me. When they wanted to know what it meant, I told them the truth: I didn't know. My father seemed pleased when I occasionally alluded to his day's work as parlaying the winner; my mother didn't seem to mind, either.

The first time I was publicly confronted by the question was in the first grade at P.S. 61. We were asked in class to verify our birthdays, addresses, parents' names, and father's occupations. It was the Depression, and I wasn't the only one in the class who didn't know what his or her father did. I joined the company of two blond-haired, blue-eyed boys with freckles who lived on Lanvale Street and a thin, dark-haired girl who was born on the Eastern Shore and wore the same sweater to school every day.

Peter Mack, one of my classmates, who lived across the street from us and was the son of a woman who had known my mother before she married my father, said to me ten minutes later, "How come you don't know what your father does? You're not that dumb." Peter's father was "in real estate." Before I could consider, I said, "I think my father is in real estate, too." I recognized instantly that I had compounded the problem and experienced a feeling which was not unfamiliar to me in my childhood—shame so powerful it seemed to me I had only one alternative with which to deal with it—never leave home again.

When I pleaded illness the next morning and begged my mother to let me stay home from school, she gave in. By late morning I was already out of my pajamas and flipping baseball cards on the living room rug with my brother. The following day my mother tested my complaint with a thermometer and the jig was up. Reluctantly, faking coughs and sighs of fatigue, I went off to school. There was no further mention of my father's occupation and Peter ignored the subject.

At school I adopted a policy of not speaking unless I absolutely had to say something. This shyness was not entirely due to my concern about my father's identity. I feared the humiliation of a wrong answer and had great difficulty understanding the mechanisms of public speech. Did you think out the sentences before you spoke? Was it possible that a teacher's recognition would be so inspiring the words would just flow? Or—and this I suspected seriously—did a lot of students have the answers to the questions before they were asked? Peter Mack was so articulate I believed he had rehearsed. (He hadn't. He and a half dozen other members of the class with whom I matriculated from the first to the sixth grades were "gifted students" with high IQs and talents that in later years enabled them to distinguish themselves as artists, physicians, university professors; one became an advisor to United States presidential candidates.)

My mother noticed my lack of enthusiasm for school and attributed it to self-consciousness about my father's work. She asked me what my response was when people inquired about my father's occupation. I told her I said I didn't know and then I confessed I felt dumb because that was the best I could do with the question. My mother suggested that the simplest answer was "the shirt business." Three of my father's five brothers—Uncles Mac, Julius, and Mike—were associated with a fourth partner, Jack Filtzer, in the Aetna Shirt Company. "If it wasn't for your father's support, there wouldn't have been a shirt business," my mother told me. "So you can feel comfortable and confident with that answer." My mother then launched a brief monologue confirming for me again what an unusual and wonderful man my father was. I welcomed my mother's admiration for my father and accepted it as true that if the qualities making him a success in his mysterious illegal business were to be directed into more conventional enterprise, he could have been a judge, general, or playing-manager of the Baltimore Orioles.

In retrospect it seems to me curious that I didn't ask at that time what precisely it was that my father did to make money. I knew he had something to do with sports, particularly horse racing, but I didn't ask my parents how the business worked. The reason for my reticence may have been my father's disdain for people who wanted to know more about him or attempted to ingratiate themselves with him with terms I later recognized as related to his work. "I'm going to Pimlico Saturday, Buckley, let me know if you have anything good." Or, "What d'you think of the price on *Omaha* in the Preakness?" My father's answer was always the same: a nod, a tip of his hat, and silence.

My mother suggested that she and I talk to my father about identifying his occupation as "the shirt business." He was sitting in the sunroom on his favorite rocker, a dark wooden piece with a worn quilted cushion and arm rests sufficiently wide for him to rest an elbow in between puffs on his Tarrytons. I remember that it was twilight because no lights were on. The *Evening Sun* flapped over one arm of the rocker and the fading light cast a dark shadow across his face. The red cigarette ash glowed like a firefly. I was grateful for the dim light because I didn't want to see his reaction. I regretted any compromise of his calm and strength and good humor.

My mother presented the situation without apology or self-consciousness. She reminded my father that children were frequently asked what their fathers did for a living. Benson and I should have an answer. My mother suggested that we say, "Shirt business."

My father rocked silently and puffed on his cigarette until I was sure the ash would fall on his chest. Mother handed him an ashtray. "What d'you think, Buck? The boys have to say something."

My father crushed the cigarette and folded his arms over his chest. He let out a deep breath. "What do I know about the shirt business, Babe?" he said. "Nothing. All I know about legitimate business is they take my money and good-bye bankroll."

"Nobody is asking you to go into another business or invest, Buck," my mother said gently. "*You* don't have to talk about the shirt business. It's just an answer for the boys, so they don't rouse more curiosity."

"It's nobody's business what I do." My father's voice expressed a bitter edge that I suspected would develop into anger. I wished my mother hadn't brought up the subject. Although my father's entire working life was spent at an activity that was against the law, he seemed to have a pathological block against saying anything that he knew was not true. I recognized his difficulty with even this harmless invention and I agreed with him that it was nobody's business how he made his living. I didn't want him to be in the shirt business and I didn't want to go to school or be with anyone else but my parents ever again.

"You do what you think is right, Lily." My father continued rocking. "The shirt business," he repeated. Then he said, "So I'm in the shirt business. My old man always said I should've been a tailor."

CHAPTER IV

Deus Ex Machina

I rarely heard urgency in my father's voice. He seemed a person who was not fazed by crisis. But when the old Philco encased in its handsome decorative oak box lost the broadcast of the Orioles game, the man who quietly experienced fortunes won and lost with the roll of dice or a close call at the finish line, petitioned for help in a rasping baritone whose distress was reminiscent of Rudolpho's final lament for Mimi.

My brother and I were profoundly impressed by my father's determination never to move the dial on the Philco once it was set. He seemed to regard dialing for stations as a talent for which only surgeons, astrophysicists, and our mother qualified. The portable Emerson in the back-room that served as the family study was available for experiments. There my mother and her sister, Jenny, listened to Texaco's broadcasts of the Metropolitan Opera. From that same magic box my brother and I heard "Cecil B. DeMille's Lux Radio Theater," "Jack Armstrong," "Terry and the Pirates," Jack Benny, Fred Allen. But the dial of the Philco was as inviolate as Hardy's "ancient performance which the sea can never claim." I was persuaded by my father's belief that the opportunity to hear the Orioles games was gift enough. It was challenging the gods who enabled voices to travel through space to manipulate the machine for other enchantments.

Benson was more dexterous and adventurous than I. He was six years old when he discovered that by intricate adjustments it was possible to pick up broadcasts from New York. Somewhere around 90, he informed me, there was a station that reported from New York City the fates of DiMaggio, Dickey, Gehrig, and Twinkletoes Selkirk.

My father's failures with the radio dial were

no less than his facility with light bulbs. When a light went out in our house we adjusted to the lack of illumination until my mother restored it. The wonder of electricity, like the miracle of sound waves travelling through space, was so mysterious and beyond his comprehension that my father had as little to do with it as possible. My mother never challenged nor criticized my father for what she cheerfully identified as his "indifference to how things work."

I had no more understanding of the radio or electricity than my father. In junior high school I made a supreme effort in science class to compensate my ma risking electrocution to bring our family light and what I perceived as her genius for "playing the radio." But all I knew about the radio was that Guglielmo Marconi sent the first long-wave signal in 1895 over a distance of more than a mile. The vocabulary—electromagnetic radiation, radio waves, amplitude modulation—was as intimidating to me as the dial was to my dad. Appreciating that Thomas Alva Edison developed the first incandescent lamp in 1879 did nothing to encourage my desire or improve my ability to find the right groove for bulb and socket. I shared my knowledge with my father. He was appreciative. "Pretty good at that," he said. "But Marconi and Edison are out of my league." I considered them out of my league, too. Although I could neither duplicate his physical courage nor emulate his talent for responding to odds, I was convinced I had inherited my father's aversion for all things scientific or mechanical, the things he lumped together as "machines."

The only "machine" with which my father had a working relationship was the family four-door Buick. Although there was mention of a Jordan in our past and his youngest brother insisted "Buckley knocked 'em dead when he rolled into Flamingo Park in a Rolls convertible" circa 1930, I don't recall my father driving any car but a four-door Buick until he was into his eighth decade. My father referred to the car as the machine or old jalopy. On hot summer nights he would suggest we pile into the old jalopy to "blow the stink off" and drive to McDonough farm for homemade ice cream. He kept both hands on the wheel when he drove and although he rarely verbalized an anxiety, his posture suggested that one false move—the slightest insensitive touch—and the jalopy would explode.

When my mother proposed that she take driving lessons, my father didn't disagree, but his demeanor clearly indicated he regarded such an adventure as a compounding of the family risk. It was not that he thought her less able than he to master the combustion machine, but two people in the same family exposed to the vagaries of engines and traffic was an unnecessary reduction of odds against catastrophe.

Dad never pretended to understand the machine—how it worked or what steps were prudent for preventive maintenance. He parked in a garage and tipped the mechanics generously to immunize the Buick against breakdowns. As he was satisfied with one station on the radio—so long as it broadcast the Orioles games—my dad required little more of his machine than that it be available for short hauls to his office, family visits, and occasional recreational outings. The only long excursions on the family agenda were two trips a summer to

Washington, D.C., to see the major league Senators entertain an American League rival. From the age of eight, my brother Benson would chart the rotations of the various pitchers and study the league's schedule before selecting the Sunday when we were most likely to see a pitchers' duel.

Bucky Harris, the Senators' manager, frequently scheduled Emil "Dutch" Leonard, the ace of the Senators' staff, for Sunday performances. From 1938, the year the Senators acquired Leonard from the Brooklyn Dodgers, to 1946, when he was shipped back to the National League Phillies, we witnessed the graceful righthander matched against the most formidable pitchers in the American League: Ted Lyons, Red Ruffing, Jim Bagby, Dizzy Trout, and Hal Newhouser. In the late summer of 1940, Leonard was having an off year. Sid Hudson was bidding to be the ace of the Senators' staff, but Harris elected to go with Leonard against the Cleveland Indians' brilliant righthander Bob Feller. Feller was on his way to a personal high of 27 wins that season and the pennant race was a three-way derby. (The De-

troit Tigers and Cleveland Indians were destined to outplay the perennial champion Yankees, with one game separating the champion
Tigers from the second-place Indians and—
could it be true?—third-place Yankees.)

There was always a sense of "history in the
making" at the major league games we attended.
No matter how remote the possibilities, my
brother and I clung to the hope of seeing a no-
hitter, or a batter hit for the cycle or . . . could
this be the year Feller would win thirty games?
Our baseball registers were filled with records
and local legends created by the recitations of
uncles and neighbors whose greatest achievements seemed to have been seeing Babe Ruth
batting at the height of his powers or Lefty
Grove mowing them down.

On the Thursday before the Sunday trip to
Washington, my dad announced that the machine would be washed and tuned-up by the
mechanic at the garage. He also reminded us of
the route—"down North Avenue to Monroe,
past St. Mary's Industrial Home where Ruth
played his first ball, and then on to Route 1 and
Griffith Stadium." Caesar planned his Gallic

Wars with no more concentration or strategy than my dad mapped our familiar advance on Washington. He took nothing for granted—gas gauge, oil gauge, tires were checked before the expedition. When the black Buick pulled up in front of 2204 Park Avenue at 9:35, Mother, Benson, and I were raring to go. Dad backed into a space in front of the house. He never double-parked and observed parking and driving regulations meticulously. We got in and my father shifted the now-gleaming Buick into gear. He moved slowly forward. There was a new Chrysler parked in front of us. From the front seat my mother said gently, "Buck, you're close to the fender."

I was aware of him making a hard left turn and then the sound of grinding steel. "Jesus," came the expletive. "I hit the bum." He shifted the car into reverse and again there was the sound of protest from the fender.

My father twisted the key and abused the gear shift. In the rear seat my brother and I sat mute and anxious. I had already abandoned the happy prospect of watching a Feller-Leonard duel. My father's anger was mounting. I saw

him glaring at the entrapped fender. His eyes
revealed no confusion—just rage. He signalled
for my mother, and my brother and I left the car
and joined her on the sidewalk.

"The fender is locked into the Chrysler's
fender," my mother said.

My father's right hand went instinctively to
his pocket—the thick roll of bills. It must have
been a major frustration that automobiles don't
respond to tips. "What we gonna do now?" he
said. Without waiting for an answer, "Call the
garage. Tell Nick there's a sawbuck waiting for
him if he gets here right away." Then he remembered it was Sunday. "Nah. Nick's off."

My mother placed a foot on the fender of our
Buick. She pressed. "It should be possible to
disengage . . . "

"Careful, Lily. Don't take any chances hurt-
ing yourself." He seemed to regard the car as an
irrational living thing that could bite or wound.
It was the moment of my childhood when I saw
my father as most helpless. I hated the car for
failing him and myself for being unable to help.
Benson, who cried even more easily than I, was
crying. I was sure this was empathy—my

brother and I sharing the same pain at observing our father as helpless. But Benson told me years later he was expressing his disappointment at missing the Senators-Indians game.

Mother had given up pressing the fender. She hitched up her skirt and crouched to make a minute inspection. It was then that Mr. Adler, our neighbor—a formal man who even at this hour of a Sunday morning was dressed in a seersucker suit, high polished shoes, and broadbrimmed panama—strolled up the avenue, double leashes in hand, walking Fritz and Fran, twin dachshunds.

Mr. Adler tipped his hat to my mother. He routinely avoided my father and did not seem the least interested in making contact now.

"Yer a mechanic, ain't you, Adler." My father's voice was accusatory. Mr. Adler was an architect but in my father's universe, all scientists, designers, mechanics, and people who dealt with machines and instruments—other than doctors—were lumped together. Before Mr. Adler could answer, my father commanded, "Come 'ere and see what you make of this mess."

Mr. Adler approached warily. He prided himself on minding his own business and allowed no compromise of good manners. From the way his eyes blinked and his shoulders suddenly stooped—as if to diminish his height advantage and excuse his capitulation—it was clear that he preferred to play no role in our family drama.

"The fenders are clearly locked," Mr. Adler said. He shrugged. The problem seemed so elementary and so easily remedied, he reconsidered his conclusion, as if there must be something more. He looked at my father, anticipating some word or visual sign that his diagnosis was accepted and his job done. My father offered no release. He stood silent, gathered to his full height, his hands pressed in his pockets. He nodded.

I have no idea what Mr. Adler, the dandy of Park Avenue and gentleman of distinguished lineage and high professional reputation, knew about my dad. I suspect he had no more than a vague idea that Mr. Offit, his neighbor, made a living violating the law. That, along with my father's gravelly voice and unconventional demeanor, made Mr. Adler suspect that acts of vi-

olence were no stranger to Buckley Offit's profession. Perhaps. I remember the look of fear
that crossed Mr. Adler's face. He blinked again,
winced, and offered the double leash to my
mother. While his cherished Dachshunds
barked and howled, Mr. Adler leapt upon the
locked fenders. He kicked and bounced,
pushed and shoved until they were disengaged.

"That should do it," he said with such great
relief that if I had not known better, it would
have seemed that he, not we, would be going
to watch the immortal Feller tested by the
contemporary jewel in the line of baseball's
Dutches.

My mother returned Fritz and Fran with a
compliment for their good behavior and gratitude for Mr. Adler's gallantry. Then, my father
with a gesture so intuitive it was predictable,
removed his right hand from his pocket and
thrust a small collection of bills at the good sa-
maritan.

"No. I couldn't," Mr. Adler protested. He
looked again at my father's eyes, the rolling
shoulders, the impatient hands. (Could it be
that he suspected that even after such a service

a casual slight could result in his execution?) It was clear that our neighbor could have been no more bewildered were he to have found himself thrust into tribal ceremonies of aborigines. He lifted his chin and stood tall, as if awaiting his executioner. "I'm sorry, Mr. Offit," he said solemnly. "I just cannot accept your money."

My father nodded matter-of-factly. "Pretty good of you at that," he said. "I 'preciate what you done for me. Maybe some day I can return d'favor."

My mother smiled. "We're taking the children to Washington today to see the baseball game," she said. We would never have made it without you, Mr. Adler."

I don't believe I or any other member of our family ever spoke to Mr. Adler again. He continued to walk his dogs but kept away from us. Feller had a no-hitter going for four innings before George Case doubled and Cecil Travis drove him home, but the Indians went on to win.

◆

CHAPTER V

Long Shots and Short Sleeves

◆ *Summer 1936* ◆

Night in the Adirondacks—my first experience away from the comforting warmth of my family. From the window of my bunk, through the branches of pine trees, I can see the sky and shadows on Schroon Lake. It seems like enough hours to fill a day have passed since our bunk's counselor, Big Ed, ended the latest installment of his narrative about Pistol Pete and Mohawk Moe—the dauntless team that survives ordeals of nature and man. Big Ed's voice, as soothing as a cat's purr, has lulled my bunkmates. I toss alone and conjure images in the dark.

I remember my father, who can sleep anywhere, anytime. "I'm gonna catch a little shut-eye, Lily. If I'm not up, give me a call in ten minutes." I am Buckley Offit. I press my eyes tight . . . "Shut-eye . . . a little shut-eye."

The silence of the night is violated by an unfamiliar bass. "So, you have the youngest of the Offit kids. Play that right, Big Ed, and his old man will make you rich."

"What'cha talking about, Dave?" It's the voice of the University of Delaware football star, my counselor. "I thought the Offits were in some kind of clothing business with your family."

"Only Howard and Morton—the good-looking Offits." He laughs. Is there other laughter? Big Ed, too? "His old man has the big bucks. He put his brothers in business."

The bass does not say my name. He had never spoken to me. I realize with sudden, terrifying clarity that he is the son of my uncles' partner. "Buck Offit is big bucks. His boy is the richest kid in this camp—by far."

Another voice—George Records, track coach, waterfront star, impresario at the piano. He once ruffled my hair and suggested I had the makings of a junior second baseman if I didn't rush the double-play pivot. "I thought Nathan Cummings owned half of Canada."

More laughter and the leaden sounds of bottles deposited on the porch steps. "And the Hechts a slice of Baltimore," the bass of Mephistopheles replies. He launches a litany of campers' names and their family fortunes. I hope the conversation will not turn again to my father, to money, to me. "Buckley Offit is the biggest bookmaker in Maryland, maybe the entire United States of America. I mean, we're talking Daddy Warbucks, Jay Gatsby, *and* Arnold Rothstein rolled into one."

"I thought Gatsby and Rothstein were one."

"Touché," replies the defiler of my father's name. "You could never tell looking at his kid, but the old man is one tough hombre. A couple years ago the Mob tried to kidnap him. He busted up a half-dozen hoods but they never got him."

A long, low whistle, and the modest, mildly embarrassed, "You don't say," of my bunk counselor.

"Oh, yeah, his brothers have nothing to do

with it—or him. This is a guy who goes it alone. There's even a story about him driving the Mob out of Baltimore. You know, he had *Jim Dandy* when he came in one hundred to one against *Gallant Fox* in 'thirty. I know that for a fact. Buck Offit gives you a tip, it's money in the bank."

It's George Records speaking now. I see him in my memory—white ducks, white tank top, tanned shoulders, thin blond hair, perfect features—athlete, musician, gentleman. "Now what did you say the business is?"

"Bookmaking. Sidney Offit's father takes bets. No limit. It's absolutely against the law. I'm surprised Bachrach even accepted him for Idylwold. I wouldn't think he'd touch that kind of money."

"Hey. Hey—" Big Ed as Pistol Pete and Mohawk Moe, too late to the rescue. "That's enough. Sid's homesick as it is. He doesn't need everybody in camp to know his father is a rich bookie. What difference does it make if he says his old man is in the shirt business?"

* * *

◆

45

From the age of ten my dad would take me to his brothers' factory at Pratt and Paca to select from their boys' line. It was the only shopping for clothes he ever did with me and he approached it with the same generosity (and impatience with indecision) he did for all choices: "Take the white and one of them blue buttondowns, too. You can make up yer mind what'cha wanna wear at home."

My uncles and their partner welcomed my father's visits and recommended shirts. "Try a half-dozen white-on-whites, Buck. They get three times our price at Hamburger's." My father seemed to consider the purchase of "bargains" a personal compromise. I suspected that he believed it a favor which, like all favors, would later be presented for reciprocity on the donor's terms. Only once did he agree to "try a reduced price box of short-sleeved madras" and that was at the urging of his brother Mike, whom he regarded with special affection. My father accepted any price but he refused to be billed and insisted on paying cash from the thick roll which he stored in his pants pockets.

This introduction to the shirt business

equipped me with a vocabulary—white-on-white, buttondown, Oxford, madras, three-ply, diversified line—to essay the subject. I made up a brief monologue and presented it to my dad. I was showing off but he didn't regard my playing at "a father in the shirt business" as in any way diminishing him. He laughed at my impersonation of a shirt salesman and credited me with "the gift of gab."

Jim Dandy—1992

After my mother died, I spoke to my father once a week. It was a routine I adopted without any particular thought, but it occurred to me soon after our conversation about Strike the Gold *that telephone contact with him required less time and effort than most good deeds. He sounded pleased to hear from me and always concluded exchanges— most often less than a minute—with regards for his grandchildren, their wives, and his great-grandchildren. He repeated each name as if reciting entries for a major stakes race.*

The week after Strike the Gold *won the Nassau County Handicap I took another shot at encouraging my dad to feel he was back in action. It required flexing the facts, but it seemed to me he*

deserved any effort I could make to help him pre-
serve his independence and feel as if he could still
make a buck. I told him we made a hundred sixteen dollars on Strike the Gold. "Not bad for a
ten-dollar bet, Pop. What d'you want me to do
with your winnings?"

My father repeated, "A hundred sixteen." There
was nothing about his voice to indicate suspicion
or disappointment, but for a man accustomed to
four-figure wagers a half-century ago my father
could hardly have been excited about a hundred
and sixteen dollars won on a long shot.

"I like Dunder Rumbles in the Jim Dandy," I
thought I heard him say. "He's gonna go off at better than twenty to one. Furusly is gonna be d'favorite."

There's a story told about my father that I first
heard when I was around eight years old. Re-
counted in various versions, it eventually became
one of the ways I came to understand his approach
to gambling. A trainer down on his luck asked my
dad to lend him a thousand dollars to bet on a
horse that was a sure thing. "I been out of action

for more than a year, Buckley, and a bunch of my pals are giving me a stake," so the legend goes. "There're six horses in the third race. My gelding is going off at seven, eight to one, and the fix is in." My father listened to this proposition, reassured himself about the details—five jockeys volunteering to throw a race so the trainer of the sixth horse could win some money. "Five guys goin' down for you," my father is reported to have said. "You don't have to borrow a thousand bucks from me to bet—you got a bet. I'm takin' yer action."

I was in Long Island the weekend of the running of the Jim Dandy Stakes. The drive from our rented cottage on Flying Point Road, Water Mill, to the OTB parlor located at a highway mall, near Southampton College, took about ten minutes. A short run, but I put it off until early in the afternoon. Thunder Rumble, the horse my father had identified as Dunder Rumbles, was going off at better than twenty to one; Furiously, an undefeated three-year-old, was the favorite. I thought about the rewards for a hundred-dollar bet if a twenty to one shot won: two thousand bucks. *I wondered if big winnings were reported to the IRS. Although my father routinely covered five-figure bets, I hadn't been to a parimutuel window more than a half-dozen times in my life, and I'd never put down even two bucks with a bookmaker or OTB. I plunked $2 on* Thunder Rumble *to win the Jim Dandy as if I was crossing the street for the first time against the light.*

CHAPTER VI

Facts of Life

◆ *Baltimore, circa 1935* ◆

It is springtime. I have just been throwing a rubber ball at the basket in the back of Sally Silverman's house on Park Avenue. The Silvermans are our neighbors. Their house seems to me a mansion because a staircase leads to Sally's bedroom on the second floor and I know there's a floor above where the maid sleeps. I am impressed by the Silvermans' large yard and the backboard and net they have inherited from a former tenant. Sally is several years younger than I, and I consider her beautiful. She has a great mass of dark hair which seems always to be gathered by a polka-dot ribbon. Her eyes have an oriental slant and she smiles a lot.

The air is filled with the smell of honeysuckle

◆

and I taste the salt flavor of a drop of my own sweat that I lick from my upper lip. The sound of adult voices resonates as if from a sound chamber. Sally says, "Daddy. Daddy is home." I follow her around to the front of the house where Mrs. Silverman is standing beneath the great arch of the entrance door—a study in soft hues of white and pink above golden meshed slippers. In my memory she is the movie actress Claudette Colbert. As the fading sun slivers through the lindens and plane trees that line the avenue, the Silvermans seem bathed in a celestial light. Mr. Silverman is wearing a gabardine suit and summer panama. A handkerchief, casually folded, flashes from his breast pocket. I hear "Welcome home, darling." Mrs. Silverman opens her tanned and perfect arms. "Dearest," says Mr. Silverman. His gabardine folds around her narrow waist. Sally moves toward her father—I am hypnotized and can hardly breathe. Before my eyes I see Mr. Silverman's and Mrs. Silverman's lips meet. It is a brief but passionate kiss. I have never seen two people kiss that way before. How old am I? Five? Six? I cannot track the year, but I flick the shutter in my memory to hold this moment forever, and then I run home filled with joy and excitement, mystery and yearning.

It is before I have seen my first movie and the only kisses I have seen are in the comic strips. (Did Winnie Winkle ever neck? Was there a moment when Terry made lip contact with the Dragon Lady?) Mr. and Mrs. Silverman in that close embrace trouble me. Why have I never seen such encounters between my parents? I ask Sally, "Does your father do that to your mother all the time?" She wants to know, "Do what?" It requires all my courage but I ask. "Kiss your mother real hard and for a long time on the lips." Sally answers with a nod and an affirmation that is almost a purr. "Uh-huh. *Ummm Hummmm.*" The sound of her voice evokes a strange, warm feeling. I think I would like to kiss Sally Silverman. But I don't. I have talked too much, and confessed to interests I'm not sure are appropriate.

Later, I tell my mother. "When Sally Silverman's father comes home from work he kisses Sally's mother right on the lips." My mother knows what I'm getting at and answers my questions. "Your father loves me just as much as Mr. Silverman cares for his wife. But your father isn't that much of a kissing man."

My mother embraced, kissed, stroked without ever seeming to use touch as a signal of approval or withdrawal. The feelings she expressed physically were as constant as the love and generosity she so tactfully shared. My father greeted us with a brief hug when he returned from work each day. His most demonstrative display of affection was the touch of his palm to my forehead when I was sick and he checked my temperature. It was as close as I can recall to a caress. It doesn't seem to me his diagnosis was ever pessimistic. Even when I was in the grip of a fever or childhood virus, my father, with his hand resting gently above my brow, would assure me, "Drink a little more water, Sid. You'll be good as new."

When I was ten years old, big for my age and showing signs of early adolescence—light growths of hair on my upper lip and "private parts"—my father seemed to feel hugs were no longer appropriate. He would jab my shoulder lightly as greeting and eventually adopted a more vigorous and not altogether pleasing tap of intimacy. If I was sitting or playing and my back was to him at a moment when he felt moved to affirm our relationship, he'd slap the back of my head and upper shoulders. More than once he would miss my head and cuff my ears so brusquely I would hear ringing and be close to tears.

I thought my father meant them as punctuations of my growing maturity and strength. It wasn't so much the pain of my father's love-taps but the injury to my dignity that I disliked. I was struggling with what I considered an excessive and perhaps abnormal sexual and romantic fantasy life. My fantasies were stimulated by our fourth-grade homeroom teacher. Miss Donaldson was a young woman of startling natural beauty. Her hair, such a pale blond it was almost white, was drawn into a bun at the back of her neck. She wore no makeup. Her casual skirts and tight blouses were so revealing that, although her academic specialty was arithmetic, to the nine-year-old boys in her charge, Miss Donaldson was a walking anatomy lesson. She was the first star of my early efforts to compose fantasy porno movies. (They progressed no further than Gothic romance.)

In a fit of chills one early spring morning, she borrowed my grey cardigan. She slipped it over her shoulders and clasped one button between her breasts. The sweater was returned to me during recess. I didn't put it on but bore it like a chalice to the yard. Philip Macht, the most worldly of my classmates, recommended I auction it to the highest bidder. I carried the sweater home in a special compartment of my school bag and put it in a drawer. There it remained as an exhibit for my studies of what I was certain were the rises in fabric that traced the contours of Miss Donaldson's breasts. My greatest satisfaction was pressing the sweater close to my nose to experience a musty but exotically sweet smell that I later associated with wet canvas but at the moment seemed to me the bodily odors of Aphrodite. Snug between the sheets I rejected my mother's good-night kiss.

I thought of Miss Donaldson—full lips slightly parted, a small chin, wide always-angry eyes. Was it possible her body was made of the same parts as the rest of us? I was unable even to imagine visual details, but I could construct a mysteriously erotic narrative.

I was less concerned about what a man and woman could do together than with whom. My fantasy affair with Miss Donaldson came to an abrupt and unromantic ending the night of open house. My mother had persuaded my father to visit the class to see a display of student work, followed by elocution hour and a brief conference with the teachers. In the twilight of late spring, it was surreal to head off to school accompanied by my mother and father. I wasn't known for the neatest papers in class and seemed incapable of listing numbers in a reasonably straight line, but my mother had me scrubbed and polished in pleated short pants, saddle shoes, and a shirt with a Buster Brown collar. I had qualified for the recitation period with "The Highwayman," and although I couldn't chart the route, I had a vague intuition that somehow this high adventure would sweep Miss Donaldson out of my fantasy and into my life. She would know—must know—she was

Bess, the landlord's daughter, the "landlord's red-lipped daughter."

It was sundown when we arrived at school and found the usually drab brick decorated with flags and bunting, crepe paper and posters welcoming our parents and celebrating the season. I stood between my parents, holding my father's hand. I was already anxious about forgetting a line or suffering the legendary blank and abandoning Mr. Noyes's hero before he could progress from canter to gallop. Miss Donaldson was at the door of our homeroom to greet us. She seemed to know Jerry Trout's father and spoke so long with Philip Macht's mother that the line was snaking to the stairwell. My mother was standing in front of me but when our turn came my father stepped forward. He was wearing a white linen suit, white-on-white shirt, navy bow-tie and wing-tipped brown and white shoes. "Rushing the season," he had said at home. It occurred to me as he presented himself and my mother to the woman of my dreams that my father was by far the most conspicuously dressed man in the school. I suspected this had something to do with money and the way he made his living. He was smoking when he spoke to Miss Donaldson, but he removed the cigarette and in a demonstration of manners I hadn't until that moment realized were even known to him, my father introduced himself. "This's Sid's mother, Lillian, and I'm 'is daddy." My father paused and smiled from the corner of his mouth in a way that I could have sworn evoked from Miss Donaldson an expression different from any I had ever seen from her before. I could only believe she was charmed or entranced by my father. "Thanks for taking care of our son for us, Sweetheart." My father employed "Sweetheart" recklessly with waitresses, maids, saleswomen. The word stunned and humiliated me. But Miss Donaldson seemed not to mind at all. She took my father's hand and didn't look at my mother or me or the hall full of well-pressed accountants, merchants, and lawyers when she said, "The pleasure is all mine, Mr. Offit. Sidney tries hard. He's a very serious little boy."

CHAPTER VII

Jim Dandy, 1930

The memory of my camp counselor's words haunted me like a wound that could be bandaged and ignored but whose scar would not go away. I could answer "shirt business" to the questions about my father's occupation but people like Dave Filtzer seemed to know more about a bookmaker's activities than I did. What did *bookmaker* mean? The word suggested something to do with the manufacture of books. But I knew that my father was not responsible for the production of my copies of the collected works of Arthur Conan Doyle or *Swiss Family Robinson*.

There had been conversations about betting, gambling, and secrecy but with the exception of my mother's concern for an answer to "Father's Occupation?" I hadn't discussed my curiosity about my father's work and its relation to society with either of my parents. When I asked the question I was twelve years old, preparing for my bar mitzvah, and consumed by an early adolescent sexuality that made me feel so adult it seemed essential that I understand all the nuances of the source of our family fortune. My mother's brother, Uncle Walt, provided the excuse for me to bring up the subject. A handsome, bull-necked insurance agent, Uncle Walt had no children of his own. He adopted Benson and me for visits to the stadium on fall afternoons to see Navy host Notre Dame or his high school alma mater City College play the Polytechnic Institute.

Uncle Walt had been a semipro baseball player, and he considered his major achievements in life to be athletic. In 1941 when I was still groping for an understanding of the rituals and economics of my father's work, I knew Uncle Walt collected premiums for the Prudential Insurance Company and earned fifty dollars a week. He and my mother were discussing a property on Park Heights Avenue which had been offered to him for two thousand dollars. He made no effort to exclude me from the conversation.

My father was due home at 5:30 for dinner. Uncle Walt joined us several times a month on Thursday evenings when his wife worked late in the millinery department of Hutzler's Department Store. He and my dad would discuss politics and sports. Uncle Walt had more information—he read the Baltimore *News Post* as well as the *Sun* and introduced me to *Life* and *Time* magazines. Nonetheless he sought my father's opinions and during the course of a long conversation, when my father would address a point or two about which he had strong feelings, Uncle Walt accepted his word as authoritative. He seemed to regard it as a compliment to be offered the predictions of a professional handicapper.

Uncle Walt was too self-effacing to ask my father directly for a loan of the money to buy the property. However, it was clear that his conversation with my mother was a solicitation for permission as well as a rehearsal. My mother said,

"Buck always has money for his brothers and God only knows how much allowance he gives his sister Ida. There wouldn't be an Aetna Shirt Company without him."

"I don't know about that," Uncle Walt said. "Jack Filtzer was in the shirt business without Buck's backing."

I heard the name Filtzer and suddenly I was reliving the day I had walked Joanne Nonningham home from the gym at P.S. 79. She had played "Moonlight Cocktail" for me on her family's old spinet and I was beginning to believe I just might live forever. In tribute to that memory, I was even prepared to forgive David Filtzer. "David Filtzer says Dad is a bookmaker," I announced to my mother and uncle.

My mother was slicing the brisket and registered no alarm. Uncle Walt turned to me with an expression of incredulity. "He said what?"

"At camp a couple years ago Dave was talking to my counselor and I heard him say, 'Buck Offit is the biggest bookmaker in Baltimore and maybe the United States.' "

Uncle Walt still couldn't believe it. "Jack Filtzer's son said that?"

"Don't make too much of it, Walter," my mother said. "He's a teenage boy trying to impress his peers. He may even resent the fact that the Offits are credited with the success of Aetna when he knows it was his father that made its shirt business possible."

"He used that word?" Uncle Walt repeated.

"He said Dad is a bookmaker. What does that mean?"

Uncle Walt shook his head. His expression indicated that I'd just had a narrow escape. "You tell them your father is not a bookmaker. Make him prove it. I have a good mind to show David Filtzer—" He raised his clenched fist and I could see the muscular arm pressing the thin fabric of his shirt.

"Buck *is* a bookmaker, Walter," my mother said. "Sidney knows his father isn't in the shirt business."

I said, "What does it mean, Ma? Why do they call Dad a bookie?"

"A bookie is a person who accepts bets on sporting events," my mother said. "You know your father takes bets on horses. You've known that since you were four years old."

Uncle Walt became suddenly composed and formal. "Lil, may I make a suggestion?" His voice assumed its courtly air. "I don't think it's appropriate for you to discuss Buck's business with Sidney. If you don't mind my saying—"

"I do mind your saying," my mother said. "And I think you should discuss this with your father, Sid. Tonight after dinner. And forget about David Filtzer. Only a person who's small and very unsure of himself tries to attract attention by trading on gossip."

The table was set and I knew my father would be home any minute. My uncle seemed so embarrassed by the discussion my mother obviously preferred to postpone it, but I had to know more. "Why is taking bets illegal?" I asked. "Just tell me that and I'll discuss the rest with Dad."

"It's the law," Uncle Walt responded quickly. "We respect the law. Your father respects the law. He's an outstanding citizen, but even fine, outstanding citizens sometimes because of various circumstances—education, poverty, limited opportunities—bend or flex laws, which they would otherwise respect . . . I'm sure Buck can explain it to you, but take my advice. He's busy. Many problems. Very difficult work. I wouldn't bother him with a question like that now."

Much as I appreciated the trips to the Stadium, the copies of *Life* and *Time,* and bacon and tomato sandwiches on toast with chocolate sodas and chocolate ice cream (the feast that preceded the football games), I was glad Uncle Walt wasn't my father. He meant well but the apologetic and illogical nature of his defense seemed unworthy of my father. My mother was no more satisfied by her brother's approach than I was. "Bookmaking is legal in Great Britain," she told me. "America has a Puritan tradition that sometimes leads to laws that are contrary to human nature and unenforceable. I'm sure your father wouldn't explain it to you this way. But taking bets on horses is no crime as far as I'm concerned. Many so-called respectable people do worse things and don't have the vice squads breathing down their necks."

"Lil—" Uncle Walt shook his head as if ridding himself of fleas.

"Sid asked a question, he's entitled to as straightforward an answer as I can give."

Later, as Uncle Walt was leaving after dinner, my mother asked him if he had discussed the loan. "Some other time," said Uncle Walt. "When you believe the time's right. Perhaps you'll ask him." Before he left he said to me in a manner as inadvertently pompous as it was fearful, "Silence is often the wisest of discretions. Remember that, Sid. I wouldn't mention that little talk we had—man to man—with your dad." My mother heard his remarks and said nothing, but before she encouraged me again to speak to my dad, she said, "Uncle Walter is a dear, sweet man but a Babbitt if there ever was one. Don't pay attention to his advice."

My father said, "I'm a bookmaker, I been one all my life. There's nothing much to it you don't already know. I take bets. If the action is too heavy and I wanna unload, I call Chicago, St. Louis, sometimes New York. What else you wanna know?"

He was sitting in the front room, smoking

and rocking. It was late fall and a window was open. The breeze billowed the flower-patterned curtain and, as was his custom, my father liked the room to be lit by a single lamp. I sat on the sofa to his right. From my position his face appeared in profile, but when he spoke he turned to me. A street lamp cast a long reddish-yellow beam through the window and blinds. He sat quietly awaiting my next question.

My father's silences were peaceful and comforting, with no trace of restlessness or the hostility I often sensed when other people didn't speak. I remember the moment because I had not prepared my questions and I sat quietly, too, studying his face. I saw the extraordinary resemblance of my father's profile to the Indian head on the nickel. It wasn't easy to flatter my father. Compliments were often the preludes to a touch and I had seen the knowing smile on his lips when a petitioner told him in exaggerated terms what a genius he had for establishing odds or how he "saved lives" by his generosity. "Yeah," my father would say. "And how much you in for?" I wanted to talk to him about money but I feared that if I didn't express myself just right my questions might seem to betray a lack of confidence in him or an effort to reinforce some false pride in myself. I felt the need to reassure him but the words which came instinctively were, "You know, you look a little bit like an Indian, Dad?"

My father smiled and said, "And so did Chief Bender but he only come up with four wins and bounced sixteen games when he pitched for the Orioles in 'fifteen."

"It's great the way you remember all the names and statistics. You could've been a terrific student, Dad."

I was less sure I wanted to talk about his business. But then my father said, "I was no good in school. I quit in the fourth grade and done what I wanted to do. Life don't owe me nothing." He paused and then he said, "So what you wanna know about the bookie business, Sid?"

I said, "I heard you're the best, Dad. You even had a horse called *Jim's Daddy,* something like that, one of the longest long shots of all time."

My father stopped rocking. He seemed vaguely amused. "Who told you that?" he said.

I said, "Dave Filtzer. I overheard him talking to another counselor at Idylwold a couple years back."

"Filtzer said that? What's that kid know? Nothin'. Most people they'll tell you this, tell you that about the gamblin' business. They think there's nothin' but money in this racket." He was quiet a moment. "I do all right," he said. "I make a living. Somebody puts down a big bet with me, they're lucky enough to hit, I pay off. A lot of wise guys, all they wanna do is collect. Comes time to pay they take a fly or wanna break somebody's legs."

My father was as discursive as I'd ever heard him. Long discourses weren't his style and I knew that although he wanted to be open and reassuring with me there was only so far he would go unless I asked him questions. I was beginning to realize I was less interested in the details of the bookmaker's operation than in some direct indication from him that he was as successful and important as he was alleged to be. I recognized the source of my curiosity as contaminated by vanity, and I knew my father wouldn't brag. I thought we had reached the end of the conversation, but then he said very slowly, deliberately, "I'm doing what I wanna do, Sid. It's my racket and I got nobody to blame or thank for it but myself. You and your brother got nothin' to worry about. Meantime, you get an education, you make up your mind how you wanna make your living. But you got plenty of time for that. People wanna talk about 'cha, they're gonna talk about 'cha. I never cared what people say about me. Only people on my list— you, yer mother, Benson. You get a little older, we'll cut it up about money. That enough for now?"

I wasn't sure I had learned anything I hadn't already known. I would have liked to ask about Rothstein. I was curious, too, about the extent of my father's wealth. But he had told me not to worry about him. He could take care of himself and us. I knew that, too, before we spoke. But I felt somehow relieved and even indifferent to Dave Filtzer and his big mouth. I was going to mention to my dad that Charlie Chaplin's *The Great Dictator* was coming to the New Theater the next week and we should plan to see it, but then my father said, "Come to think of it that horse *was Jim Dandy.* Beat *Gallant Fox,* paid one hundred to one. Pat McGovern had him. I had a piece of it."

CHAPTER VIII

Best of Friends

Although my father seemed to have a regiment of admirers and petitioners as well as business associates, I don't recall a friend of his ever having a meal at our house. With the exception of my mother's former colleague Anne Rosenthal, a Saturday evening visitor who discussed books, movies, and fashion with her, my parents' social life was restricted to their families.

From the age of six I accompanied my father to Sunday doubleheaders at the old Oriole Park. The Birds, an International League team at the time, hosted major league farm clubs, among them the Newark Bears, Rochester Red Wings, Toronto Maple Leafs, Syracuse Chiefs, and Montreal Royals. We always sat toward the third base side of home plate. We'd frequently progressed no further than the turnstile or the walk across the concrete underpass when my father was accosted by a petitioner.

The dialogue always ended with my father passing a few bucks and a line of personalized philosophy, "Don't play too many long shots, Monty. Put it in the bank." Among the legion of dandies, fops, and sporting bloods who visited my father during the game, invariably someone was determined to buy me a special treat. My instructions were specific: "Take nothin' from nobody." Nonetheless, the admiration the third-base regulars accorded my father converted more than one afternoon at the ballpark into a testimonial.

I was particularly fond of Bibbish, an aging gentleman who wore a fading seersucker suit and straw hat and insisted upon slipping pennies into my trouser pockets even as my father was staking him to a few dollars. I remember, too, a former jockey named Smallfry who wore a golf cap pulled low over his eyes and never seemed capable of a sentence beyond, "Anything good today, Buckley? Got anything good?"

Sometimes Sad Sam would sit by my father's other side. He, too, was a quiet man but his expression was radiant, as if he had just heard a hilarious joke or was so pleased to see us he couldn't contain his joy. Unlike the other citizens of Oriole Park who approached my father, Sad Sam didn't seem in need of favors or money. He knew all the ushers and could deliver an autographed baseball on request.

It wasn't until a quarter of a century later that I realized Sad Sam was the source of my greatest triumph as a fan. On a trying Sunday afternoon for the home team when Buddy Rosar and Charley Keller of the Newark Bears were demonstrating their claims to a place with the major league Yankees, Sad Sam handed me the scorecard with the day's lucky number. I had no idea that "the fix was in," and rejoiced at the stroke of luck that brought me five dollars' worth of free cleaning at Old Line Laundry, a bouquet from Mason-Dixon flowers, a box of Fanny Farmer chocolates, and a three month's subscription to the *Sporting News*.

All my father's friends and acquaintances had nicknames. The monikers denoted personal eccentricities or, more often, the reverse of obvious features. Fat Freddy was so thin he appeared anorexic and Slim Sammy must have suffered a glandular disorder that would account for his three hundred pounds. My father's tone and demeanor when he addressed these lesser lights of Baltimore's sporting scene was affectionate and respectful. Aristotle strolling the Lyceum of ancient Athens, discussing justice or reasons for being, was no more of a peripatetic philosopher than my father on Sundays at Oriole Park, passing along odds and gambling shibboleths as well as practicing that special brand of fraternal philanthropy he called a "grub stake."

Rarely did he impose upon any of his acquaintances for a service or act of friendship. An exception was the day I was released from Mt. Sinai Hospital after an appendix operation. It was the day before the Preakness, a high holiday in my father's profession. He delegated Moody Max, a six-foot-two, elegantly dressed sport, to pick me up and take me home from the hospital. Moody Max arrived in a blue blazer, white ducks, and panama to lift me from the hospital bed. He seemed to me a charming and sophisticated fellow reminiscent of Cary Grant. I knew he was a former boxer, and I was grateful to him forever for addressing me as "Champ."

My father's best friend, partner, and only confidant was Willis "Buzz" King. During the years of my early childhood, before my brother was old enough to join us, my father frequently brought me along on morning visits to Mr. King's small estate in the country. When I was an adult and writing a novel about a Baltimore bookmaker, I had several long interviews with Buzz. It was then I learned that he was the grandson of a St. Louis gambler who had travelled to California, where he opened a casino catering to prospectors. Buzz's father had followed the family "calling," but Buzz had left the West in his teens and moved to Baltimore to make his fortune sponsoring private, high-stake crapshoots and card games. He met my father on the streets of downtown Baltimore soon after World War I. Their association was based on trust and an undefined but shared belief that in the business of gambling—squeezed between the odds and the law—there was an advantage in a joint operation.

My father did the bookmaking, took the bets, hired the agents, collected, paid off, and was responsible for connections with a network of bookmakers throughout the country with whom he could lay off or share when action was particularly heavy on a race. Buzz set up the private high-stakes games—cards or craps—and from time to time invested in and managed clubs that fronted for the backdoor gambling operation.

Of course I knew none of this when our old Buick pulled up to Mr. King's driveway in the mid-thirties, and we were greeted by the tall country gentleman with the leonine head. Frequently he dressed in shooting knickers and high boots.

Mr. King had no children of his own. (He was married twice. His second wife was the widow of Baltimore's former police commissioner.) He greeted me as a peer, with nothing in his manner to indicate he recognized that I was a child. It was as if he considered me an extension of my father, for whom he had great respect and an as yet undefined love. Beyond the driveway of Mr. King's house was a kennel which housed a half-dozen hunting dogs, all straining at the leash and barking furiously. The walls of the study in which I amused myself while my father and Mr. King conferred were decorated with the heads of great elk and a bear and an arsenal of hunting rifles.

I was offered carte blanche to Mr. King's collection of pistols, dice, cards, roulette wheels, and sheathed hunting knives. It was a measure of my father's confidence in me that he only cautioned me once about playing with the guns. I recall amusing myself with various sets of dice. When he was aware of my selection, Mr. King would say, "Shake them up good, Sid, if you don't come up with two sevens every ten rolls, you get your money back."

The last time I visited him, Buzz was dying of cancer. He appreciated my attention and, although a guarded and quiet man, treated me to a long monologue on his career that included a citation of my father as "The best there is or probably ever will be. Buckley never talks himself into any bet or second-guesses himself." I was startled when he ended that compliment with the suggestion that if the business had been legitimate my brother Benson could have inherited it and been " . . . almost as good as Buckley. But not you, Sid. I could tell when you were knee-high you were more interested in looking around and taking it all in than figuring the odds on those craps."

After we left the hospital that day I asked my father why Mr. King and his wife never came to our house. I wondered if there was a reason why my parents never socialized. "The less people know, the better," was my father's response. "Somebody sees us in a restaurant, cutting up a pot, drops it to some gabby, the next thing you know they have a knock on us." There was no sense of regret or sacrifice in this explanation. My father seemed to accept it as a cost of doing business that the depth of his association with Buzz be known only to the two of them.

My mother, too, endorsed this backstreet partnership. Although she expressed fondness for Buzz and both his wives, to whom she had only occasionally talked on the phone, she accepted my father's insistence on self-imposed isolation.

This passion for privacy made for one of the major tensions of my childhood. My father's notion of a perfect day off was to sit quietly in his rocking chair in the sunroom of our apartment on Park Avenue and later Lake Drive. He seemed to regard uninvited guests as busybodies or people in quest of a handout. These suspicions were well-founded. During the last years of the Depression I recall unannounced visitors—distant relatives or remote acquaintances—ringing our bell because they "were in the neighborhood and decided to drop in." The brief visits were always terminated when my father stuck his hand in his pocket and brought out a contribution to their "bread basket."

On more than one occasion he spotted a potential intruder on his way down the avenue. He would spring from the rocker, close the blinds, and turn out the lights. We huddled in the backroom until three minutes after the doorbell rang.

My mother expressed few complaints about

my father but from time to time she would re-
mark on the sparseness of their social life. Yet
she framed the complaint as a compliment,
"Your father is a very wise man. He realizes that
a successful bookmaker is vulnerable to jeal-
ousy or gossip. I don't really mind giving up the
company of other people for my Buckley." But it
was obvious she did feel isolated if not exactly
lonely.

CHAPTER IX

Club Night

◆ *Winter 1945* ◆

Club night at the Valley Forge Military Academy, Wayne, Pennsylvania. It is three months since General MacArthur accepted the Japanese surrender on the battleship *Missouri*. General Patton has died in a Heidelberg army hospital. Charles de Gaulle has been elected president of France. In grey uniform with starched white collars and cuffs, shoes shined to a high gloss, three—only three—cadets turn out for the first meeting of the corps literary club. Our advisor—a weary veteran of the Battle of the Bulge—invites us to loosen our collars and "talk about anything that's on your mind."

I am in my third and final year at the Forge, a

refuge for young men "in need of discipline,"—
army brats, aspiring West Pointers, and sons
who for various reasons are served by the anonymity of a uniform. The protocols of the drill
field are contagious—in classrooms, too, cadets defer to rank. I wear the stripes of a cadet
master sergeant. Is it possible that not one cadet
officer is interested in literature?

Exercising the privilege of my rank for the
first time in a cadet assembly, I say, "I've just
read Richard Wright's *Black Boy.* It's a very
important book. The most important work of
fiction of our time. Wright's autobiographical
approach testifies to the fact that—" I pause for
dramatic effect, struggling for Clifton Fadi-
man's style and the elusive cliché of command—"American justice will never work until
we are fair to the negroes." I conclude with a
quotation from the review I am writing for the
Legionnaire campus weekly, "*Black Boy* is a
must-read."

The veteran nods, yawns. "Anyone else read
any good books lately?" From the row behind
me comes a voice whose diction connotes the
authority of what in the jargon of our school is

identified as "upper crust." I have encountered such voices from time to time at Valley Forge. They are usually those of the rebellious sons of distinguished families who have exhausted the patience of Exeter, Andover, Milton, Lawrenceville, or the Hill. They arrive at this academy less concerned than their parents that Valley Forge can "mold men from boys."

"I've been reading Orwell's *Animal Farm*." Did I hear him say in a British edition? "Satiric, of course, but a brilliant representation of man's demonstrable inability to construct anything like an equitable society." He speaks on, tracing the story line, defining the symbolism of the characters, discoursing on the evils of totalitarianism from the right or left or even that which "creates artifice and liturgy to dominate little boys."

I don't hate this school. My father has said, "It's up to you. I know nothin' about schools. I never got past the fourth grade." The war was on; a neighbor suggested to my mother that if I wasn't accepted at McDonough, a semimilitary school in Pikesville, Valley Forge might "give

Sidney more confidence." I'm pleased with the lack of academic competition, the availability of cadets for games, the company of delinquents from New Jersey, true-believers from Donora, Pennsylvania, and royalists from Latin America. I'm satisfied with life at a military school and yet the half-dozen cadets with whom I share my deepest intimacies all detest the place. The tall, red-faced cadet has told the literary club that our school "creates artifice and liturgy to dominate little boys" and for me that's an invitation to friendship.

Our advisor glances at his watch, the desk, the earnest eyes and acned faces of his command. He mentions the possibilities for a literary magazine—reviews, stories, poems. Do we want to write? But what to write? The wearer of the combat infantry badge repeats our names in alphabetical order: "Lewis, Murphy, Offit." His tone mellows, "Why don't you write about your father, Lewis. I'm sure we'd all be interested in him." Lewis rises. He snaps to attention, the red face is flushed, the cropped blondish-red hair seems electrified with rage. "I will not, Sir. This

is a voluntary activity. I attended because I believed—obviously erroneously—that I might
write poetry."

"Of course. Write what you want. It doesn't
even have to rhyme." A forced chuckle. "I've obviously disturbed your muse. No offense meant.
How about you, Offit—" He has turned to
me—out of alphabetical order!—"Why don't
you write a short piece about *your* father." Is it a
rhetorical question? A plea for support because
I am, after all, the ranking cadet? A genuine
groping to get us started? Or—I can't fully as-
similate the meaning and consequences of the
alternative—does he know? Is the anonymity of
the uniform a deception? I'm wounded, but less
defiant than Lewis. "I'd rather not, Sir. I've been
planning to write a short story." The situation
arouses my adrenaline and I compose the out-
lines of a tale that involves " . . . the twin sister
of a cadet who dresses in her brother's uniform.
The daughter of the academy superintendent
falls in love with her under the mistaken impression she is the handsomest, gentlest member of the corps. In the meantime her brother,
who drapes himself in his sister's clothes, ar-

rives on campus and is promptly intercepted and wooed by the cadet captain . . . "

I go on, until our advisor interrupts. "Don't talk it out, Offit. Get it down for critique next meeting." He pauses and then with one of those sudden bursts of erudition displayed by military faculty when we least expect it, he recommends, "You may want to take a look at *Twelfth Night*. It was taken from 'The History of Apolonius and Silla' in 'Richie, His Farewell to the Military Profession.' "

I don't smoke but I amble to the butt area with Lewis who is wearing the insignia of a trooper. He doesn't seem entirely to focus on me, but he likes to talk and responds with surprise and gratitude when I tell him how much I admire his critique of *Animal Farm*. We stand under the winter sky. He exhales smoke and I, frosted breath. We seem bonded by our religion of words, a minority—not quite persecuted but alien within the regiment of cadets. We must have an intimacy, a secret to seal our new friendship. I ask him why he was so enraged by the suggestion he write about his father. His eyes test my motive. He lets out a long stream of smoke through his nostrils. "My father is Sinclair Lewis, you know. He's my real father. Of course, I could have written about Mother's current husband. He's an artist. A good fellow, really. But he doesn't need the publicity either." Lewis laughs, and I join him. I don't know why we are laughing. Sinclair Lewis? I know he's a writer. That's all I know. But if we're friends I can ask, so I do. "Is he a famous writer?" Without pride or irritation Lewis tells me, "My father won the Nobel Prize for literature. When he won a Pulitzer he wouldn't even accept it." He crushes his cigarette and lights another with such urgency it's difficult to believe he can survive the smoking bans at Valley Forge. "My mother is a writer, too. Dorothy Thompson. But I don't want to talk about it. I don't like talking about my parents. Once it's in the air, that's all anybody ever wants to talk to me about. There. I told you. We're fellows in letters and must be honest with each other. Now—what about you? Why won't you write about your father?"

I've never told anyone my father's occupation. It's the secret that protects my family from strangers. "I told you," Michael Lewis repeats.

There's something about his voice that tells me he's familiar with betrayal. He doesn't share confidences easily. I mustn't fail him. He's told me his father won the Nobel Prize, and I'm thinking it's a subject he doesn't wish to discuss even though it's not a family secret. I tell him I've never smoked, but I'd like to smoke a cigarette with him now. It's an offering—to substitute for the confession he believes he deserves, but I'm unable to share.

He offers me a cigarette. "Christ, what is it about your father. Does he beat you with a cat-o'-nine-tails? Or is he Billy the Kid?" I laugh and tell him his use of language is the most inventive I've ever heard.

"I'm not accustomed to compliments. And what's worse, I'm sure you mean it." He laughs again, fidgets awkwardly. He's the tallest cadet in the butt area and I have the sense that others who are familiar with him regard his movements and moods as peculiar. A cadet I know passes us without speaking but points to Lewis and twists his index finger to his temple.

"Recite something you've written," I say.

He seems to have forgotten my father. He recites. The poem doesn't rhyme. I'm not sure I understand his meaning, but I'm not paying close attention. The familiar notes of tattoo remind us taps is not far behind. He offers to recite again. There are no other cadets in the butt area and I'm risking bed check and demerits, but I owe him this. He's caught in the spell of his words and he's even more an actor than I. When there's a pause I tell him he must be the president of our literary club. A tactical officer reminds us "The smoking lamp is not lit." Michael snuffs out his cigarette. He seems exhilarated. Before we part, he grasps my shoulder tightly. "Next time I want to hear all about your father and those cat-o'-nine-tails, Offit. Is it a promise?"

"A promise," I say.

I'm the tenth cadet on the junior-varsity basketball team. We practice every club night. The next time I see Michael Lewis is backstage at a Broadway theater fifteen years later. He's performing in an eighteenth-century military costume. Of course he remembers me, he says. "Didn't we recite poetry together?"

CHAPTER X

Chance

Only once did my father identify a horse in which he had a bettor's interest. In the early spring of 1947, when I was a freshman at Johns Hopkins, he told me I should root for a thoroughbred named *Phalanx.* "I took a flyer in the winter line," my father said. "He's lucky enough to win the Derby, we win a package." My father registered as much excitement as I had ever seen him show for a sporting event. He didn't define his stake in the result and I didn't ask him, but when he discovered the afternoon of the race that I was on my way to an early evening party with friends from the Hopkins, he reminded me to root for *Phalanx.*

I was sitting deep in a bale of hay with one

arm around Carol Abramson and both ears attentive to a portable radio when I heard the call—"It's *Phalanx*—*Phalanx* by a nose." Then, an incredible moment in sports broadcasting, the announcer confessed he had misread the colors. The winner of the 1947 Kentucky Derby was *Jet Pilot,* Eddie Guerin up. I felt grief approaching tragic loss. If my father mentioned a "rooter's interest" the stakes must have been very high. As soon as a telephone was available I called home. My father seemed surprised, even embarrassed by the call. "That's horse racing," he said, and then repeated another of his soothing clichés, "You gotta take the bad with the good." Many years later he recalled that his "information" had been so authoritative, he had plunked down two thousand dollars at twenty-to-one. *Phalanx* won the Belmont, New York's Derby, that year. I was sitting with my father, who was rocking in his familiar chair to hear the call. He said nothing that indicated he resented this belated victory. It was just another horse race as far as he was concerned.

During my years at the Hopkins, with what I considered my newly acquired analytic tools, I

tried to examine my father's philosophy as it related to gambling. This effort was encouraged
when an associate philosophy professor at the
Hopkins, Albert L. Hammond, spoke openly of
his affection for betting on horse races and de-
fended it as consistent with what he considered
the "purposely purposeless" order of the universe. As he developed his thesis, Dr. Hammond told us: "Any good gambling house
demonstrates the truth of this idea. This is not
to make it all simply luck. Gambling houses
take cuts on the horses as well as offer roulette.
The house will give you a ride back to town and,
if a good house, will give you a five dollar bill if
you go broke—to buy you dinner and get you
home. I like to think the universe is as kindly."
The tributaries of Dr. Hammond's river of ideas
often left me baffled and humble, but he was
the only person in all my education who suggested a relationship between my father's work
and the riddles that briefly but intensely engaged me—Where did we come from? Where
are we going? What is the purpose of it all? He
suggested that gambling was the logical extension of free enterprise as well as a flirtation with

chance and luck, sources instrumental in the shaping of the universe and man's destiny.

I was so impressed by Dr. Hammond's discussions I shared some of his ideas with my father. He smoked and rocked and nodded and told me, "The professor is a better talker than he is a handicapper." That was my only clue that Dr. Hammond, too, contributed to the shoeboxes stored in the wall above our family shower.

My father, as Dr. Hammond's thesis suggested, viewed the universe as a great gambling casino and although he never composed sentences to define a philosophy, his responses to the tragedies, joys, paradoxes, and choices of life were consistently infused with gamblers' references. "You're born in the United States of America, you beat the price of geography and history." When our children were born he expressed no preference or even concern about gender. "They got ten fingers and ten toes and a clean bill of health, you got a winner." He regarded his own fortune as another of life's lucky breaks and believed it a disrespect to the Lords of Chance to refuse a petitioner's request. "Live and let live," he would say. My father indulged in no self-pity—ever. He considered himself a winner. "Life don't owe me nothing," was among his most constant refrains.

I had difficulty reconciling his unromantic, rather soulless pragmatism with the ideas that most attracted me. Pantheism, neo-Platonism, even the mysticism of Judaism and Christianity were much more intriguing to my imagination. Gambling neither tempted nor satisfied me, but for the two most important decisions of my life I played against the odds and took the risk. When I told him I wanted to make a living as a writer, my father asked me what I thought the odds were of ever making a living at my kind of bookmaking. "A hundred to one," I said. "Okay," was his reply. "But only go broke once." And two years later, when I eloped with Avodah Crindell Komito, age nineteen, he wanted to know if I could support a wife. I had no sense of money but was so full of the power of love, I was sure I could support the world. "You're an entry," my father said in a surprisingly intuitive perception of Avi's talents and our relationship. "That gives you two shots instead of one. Sometimes you gotta play a hunch."

Thunder Rumble— 1992

"Rank Outsider Rescues the Jim Dandy Stakes," was the headline. In his special dispatch to the New York Times, August 3, 1992, Joseph Durso wrote, "In racing's celebrated house of upsets, chalk up one of the biggest. Thunder Rumble, a 24-to-1 outsider who had raced once in five months outran some of the elite 3-year-old colts in the country today and won the Jim Dandy Stakes by half a length over Dixie Brass, and in an upset within an upset the undefeated colt Furiously ran fourth . . . it attracted a glittering field of eight and a throng of 37,204 fans to the Saratoga Race Course . . . they watched in wonder as an interloper defeated the favorite, equaled the stakes record for the Jim Dandy, and paid $51.80 to any-

body smart enough or bold enough to bet $2 on him."

That evening I called my father in Baltimore and told him we'd hit the jackpot. "I bet the hundred bucks you won on Strike the Gold *on* Thunder Rumble, *Pop. It's a parlay good for over two thousand dollars." There was a long silence on the other end of the phone. I'd never deliberately lied to my father, but I knew he was having difficulty coming to terms with the probability of me making the bets. "Two thousand five hundred ninety dollars, Dad—it looks like you're on a roll."*

"Pretty good at that," was my father's response. There was nothing about his tone of voice to indicate excitement or pleasure. "He win by half a length at a mile an eighth, he runs the Travers, two, three weeks from now, the price is right—go with 'im at a mile and a quarter."

I said, "OK, Dad, we'll see about that. Meantime you want me to send you the twenty-five hundred?" Twenty-five hundred dollars seemed a modest gift when I considered the bills paid by Benson and Suzie, but I hadn't expected my father to risk his run of luck. It seemed extraordinary that after a lifetime as the "house," in his tenth decade he was handicapping the stake races and playing his hunches—with me as his agent.

"You hold on to the bankroll, Sid," he said. "You lay down the bets, I'm dead and gone, split d'pot with yer brother."

"You're not going anywhere, Pop," I said. "You sound great—and just let me know a couple days in advance if you want me to hit OTB for the Travers." I tried to get him going about the fading Orioles and listless Mets but his last words were, "That Dix Brassy's a helluva speed horse—whadda I know? Only what I read in d'papers with my good peeper."

I didn't think much about the Travers Stakes or this spontaneous role change that had me—a person who neither analyzed odds nor gambled—booking to my own father. It seemed an easy way to boost his spirits and redistribute the family "wealth," but it did cross my mind that if Thunder Rumble went off at better than 2–1 and my father's luck continued, my father's legacy could grow to a five-figure "bundle."

CHAPTER XI

Tell It to the Marines

◆ *Towson/Brooklyn/Baltimore 1951* ◆

A grey summer morning, 8 A.M.; I'm on my way to report to the G2 of the Brooklyn Army Base, the port of embarkation from which supplies and personnel flow to support the United States cadre in western Europe. This month the federal jury in New York has indicted twenty-one Communist Party leaders for conspiracy to teach and advocate the overthrow of the United States government by force and violence. A fellow officer of the reserve unit for the Baltimore Port, with which I am training, tells me: "There's a story in today's *Sun* about a gambling raid. My wife, who called this morning, says one of the men arrested is named Offit."

◆

The captain, a judge advocate, is unlikely to have invented this item. Even less likely is it that the Offit of whom the captain's wife reports is Uncle Eddie, the only other among the dozen Offit men living in Baltimore who might have been nabbed in a gambling raid. I'm tempted to ask my informant, a practicing attorney, about the penalties for such violations of the law, but determine to deny him the flattery of my curiosity. I remind him there's a distinguished family living in Towson and often confused with us. I neglect to tell him that they spell their name "Offutt."

I am the only member of the reserve unit who has been fully investigated and approved for top-secret clearance. My age—twenty-two—and long association with the army reserve, including attachment to an intelligence unit during the years of ROTC, qualify me for this apparitional distinction. It is the era of McCarthyism and even though, in my last editorial for the Johns Hopkins *Newsletter,* I have lamented "the conviction of Alger Hiss on the good faith of a paranoid"—even though I have mocked my classmates for "standing in uni-

formed greys and black knit ties to applaud
daintily for our noble Owen Lattimore," for the
moment I am the only certified, Joe McCarthy-
proof, true-blue American among the members
of our reserve unit and, for all I know, the con-
stabulary of the Brooklyn base. With such cre-
dentials I don't feel obligated to respond any
further to hearsay about a gaming raid in Baltimore County that I immediately know means
my father has been nabbed for his lifetime occupation.

Since graduation from college in 1950, with
the money I earn from stories sold to pulp
magazines—westerns, sports, mysteries at a
half-cent a word—and the several thousand
dollars I earn each year for attending weekly reserve meetings and summer camp, I am on my
own, living in an upper-west-side one-room
walkup with bath down the hall. I am in touch
with my family often and believe that as a result
of the Kefauver Congressional hearing on crime
my father has quit the bookmaking business. I
decide not to call him until evening.

I report to the G2, a beefy, balding lieutenant
colonel, whose face is committed to a perpetual

smile but who speaks in long, rambling mono-
logues on a variety of subjects all of which are
designed to convince me that America is
doomed unless we quickly mend our ways. "The
Rosenbergs are the tip of the iceberg. . . . Truman was loony to dismiss MacArthur. . . . Race
riots in Chicago are an omen of anarchy . . . "
But the special passion of my commander's
scorn is evoked by Harry Bridges, president of
the International Longshoreman's and Ware-
houser's Union, a West Coast organization that
the colonel informs me is a "hotbed of communism." The career and menace of Harry Bridges
is narrated by the colonel with a smile that suggests he can barely contain an outburst of
laughter. I have not quite grown accustomed to
this counterpoint of style and substance and am
waiting for the punchline. At the same time I'm
thinking of my father and wondering how long it
will be before the colonel learns that his top-
secret confidant is the son of an arrested
bookie. I hold fast to my father's cliché as scripture, "Don't worry about what people say about
you. You got nobody to satisfy in this world but
yourself."

The colonel finishes by reminding me that although the government's efforts to deport Harry Bridges as a communist alien failed (Bridges was born in Australia but became a citizen of the United States in 1945), he's been convicted and sentenced to prison for perjury for denying Communist Party membership. I wonder if my father will take the stand in his own defense. I've never heard him lie. He seems incapable of even a white lie or evasion. When confronted by a question to which he doesn't wish to respond, my father remains silent. Silence is his fortress and he retreats to it with confidence and calm.

My duty for the day is to continue probing the files of names of merchant seamen scheduled to depart the Brooklyn base to find those who have been associated with the West Coast union. This procedure requires me to run a metal rod through a file of cards, elevate it, and check the names of ILWU members that appear against the roster of crewmembers due to sail to Bremerhaven, West Germany. The file has been so coded that no other information is available from this simple thrust. If I want to learn the age, family history, or experience of the crewman, I'd have to conduct a personal interview. The colonel trusts me to determine during the conversation whether I consider the union member a sufficient security risk to bar him from sailing. When he explains this charge to me the colonel is surprisingly sympathetic to those he considers "naive workingmen, probably good Americans who didn't have a virgin's chance in a whorehouse of understanding what Harry Bridges is up to." He doesn't seem to recognize that this suggestion is somewhat contradictory to his previous announcement that the union was a "hotbed of communism."

Although I consider myself reasonably enlightened about current events, I have never heard the name Harry Bridges before the colonel assays his career, but he is fast becoming for me the workingman's Alger Hiss. During the first days of my assignment I consider it a great adventure to meet the seamen and deckhands whose union leader advocates the overthrow of our government.

Before I learn of my father's arrest, I identify these vigorous, blunt-spoken men with him. They have neither his stature nor unique intelligence, but the words of gratitude they speak to the United States are reminiscent of my father's own deeply felt patriotism. I accept their explanations and bar no one from passage. The colonel has not commented on my permissive policy. When he tells me that the men to whom I speak are dependent upon these jobs for the support of their families, I'm not certain whether he's rationalizing the standards of his top-secret protégé or confessing his own misgivings about depriving men of their livelihood.

That evening I call my parents. My father picks up the phone after one ring. Nothing about his voice suggests he's irritated or anxious. He greets me with his usual cheer and tracking of the pennant race. "Looks like you'll have the party all to yourself in New York." It occurs to me that my father thinks that because I'm out of town I can escape any relationship to the report. I'm cautious about saying anything that may suggest exaggerated concern. I don't have to wait long. In a low rasp my father asks, "Anybody knock to you about me being picked up in the county?" I tell him one of the officers has mentioned it. "Don't worry about it," my father says. "I'm taking care of it. Any-body asks you, you tell them you know nothing about it."

I realize without his telling me that my father does not want to discuss such private matters on the phone. He assumes his line may be tapped and although he doesn't allow this suspicion to govern all his calls, this is a moment for special caution. My mother seems less daunted, but the words she speaks to me indicate that she, too, believes the line is tapped and she speaks to the eavesdropper as if to a jury. "All this fuss about people placing bets on horses is ridiculous. If your father wanted to make money on a horse-race he'd go to the track." I fall into the rhythm of my mother's performance and speak briefly of the important work I am doing to protect our nation against communism. But I cannot resist mimicking Senator McCarthy and soon my mother and I are sharing a laugh without identi-fying the pleasure we are taking in paranoia.

Three days before the completion of the train-ing tour, a senior officer of the Baltimore unit asks me what is my relationship to the Offit who works for his old friend Pierre Fernier. I have never heard the name Pierre Fernier before and I tell him so. "Fernier was running a gambling house from his farm in the country," the major tells me. "According to the Baltimore *Sun* Buckley Offit was arrested with him last week." My impulse is to inform the major that my father works for no one. I experience a flush of pride and even egoism about my father's reputation. I want to repeat the words of my camp counselor which had distressed me when I was a child but now seem an appropriate testimonial: "Buck Offit is the biggest bookmaker in Maryland, maybe the entire United States of America." It's a vanity I know my father would not endorse, but I'm offended that this superior officer believes Buckley Offit, whom he doesn't know, works for his friend. I shrug and say nothing. He asks, "What relationship is this Offit to you?"

I look directly into the wide, not unkind eyes and answer, "Buckley Offit is my father, Sir."

"Well, tell him to watch himself with Fernier. Pierre's a real sport but a lousy farmer who drinks too much and is destined to wind up a millionaire or hanged."

I'm burning now to tell the major that my father's fate is tied to no other man. Buck Offit can take care of himself in Baltimore County or any other place in the world. He needs no advice. But I say nothing. The major winks and pops my shoulder, "Remind me never to play cards with you, Offit." I smile, uncertain if it's a dig or a compliment.

The last day of my training I'm sitting across the table from Marco Mullin, a tanned, grey-haired seaman whose card has made him a candidate for a security risk. I'm down to my last hours to find a "communist" to bar from a merchant crew. Mullin's posture is erect but his body is so tense, his slightest movement makes me think he's about to spring from his seat and attack me. Mullin has responded to the routine questions about his name, address, years of service with more hostility than I would have believed possible for a man to achieve with the repetition of his own name. When I ask if he's a member of the ILWU, he says, "Positively." I inquire as to his familiarity with Harry Bridges, and he tells me he's heard Mr. Bridges speak. "Harry Bridges is nobody's fool. He knows who is exploiting who in this country. Who has who's finger up who's asshole."

I have had no previous experience with a suspect of Mullin's passion and candor, but I continue as if all is normal. I ask Mullin if he's aware that Harry Bridges has been convicted for perjury for denying he is a member of the Communist Party. Mullin answers, "What's wrong with that?" I try another tack: "You're not a member of the Communist Party, Mr. Mullin, are you?"

"Absolutely." Mullin's grey hair composes a wreath around his bald head. He has a neat grey mustache, too. I'm color-blind, but I know his eyes aren't brown; they may be blue-grey or green. I wonder about his national origins. He's certainly not an ethnic "type."

"Where did you say you're from, Mr. Mullin?" I was going to ask where he was born, but I suspect the insinuation would only further cloud the issue.

"I been born and bred in Salinas County and worked for every damn thing I eat or drink or put on my back. Nobody ever give me anything for nothing and that goes for my wife and kids, too. You got that straight?" Mullin pauses. No expression I can manage will put him at ease or temper his anger. He leans forward and jabs a finger in my direction. "Let me tell you something, Lieutenant . . . Boy. I am old enough to be your father and I am here to tell you there is going to be some serious changes in this country. You get that? *Comprende? Cupire? Haben sie es vernommen?* The workingman is not going to be exploited by a gang of plutocrat capitalists working hand in hand, in cahoots with their puppets in Washington. And it is communism gonna change all that. You wasting your time and mine pussy-footing around. I am speaking communism and yours truly is for it one hundred and ten percent." Mullin nods his head, vigorously endorsing his own statement. He seems to be sitting without the help of the chair now, but his back remains straight, shoulders square, neck extended.

I'm beginning to feel that Mullin is trying to intimidate me into violating some higher moral code. I shrug and slap the desk. "One thing more, Mullin. The United States Army, the government, certainly don't want to deprive you of the means by which you support yourself and your family. When you ship out, you don't intend to—" this I pass off with another forced smile—"you're not going to be making speeches advocating the violent overthrow of the United States government. Are you?"

Marco Mullin declares, "That is exactly what I intend to do. How else you gonna have a change without revolution? You think them capitalists in Washington just gonna hand it to you?" It's Mullin who's struggling now. He lifts his hands and drops them to his thighs with an expression of frustration reminiscent of an earnest teacher in the company of a hopeless student.

A long silence follows. Mullin and I lock eyes. It reminds me of an adolescent contest— the loser is the one who smiles or flinches first. Marco Mullin opens and closes his eyes quickly several times. We both know we have nothing more to say to each other, but Marco Mullin cannot possibly know that I'm not in a frame of mind to convict anyone of anything. I haven't aspired to be judge or jury. I stand, offer my hand and say, "Bon voyage, Mr. Mullin." Mullin rises and clutches my hand. His grip is so tight I have to release all tension from my fingers to keep him from crushing the bones. When he's at the door I add, "I guess this is what America is all about."

Marco Mullin sucks in his breath and shakes his head as if I and the entire United States are hopeless. His last words to me are, *"Cuentaselo a tu abuela!*—tell it to your grandmother—tell it to the Marines."

CHAPTER XII

The Fix—Fact or Fiction

I returned to Baltimore courtesy of the USAR on a Saturday afternoon. My father wasted no time getting right to the point. He told me about the raid and defined his relationship to Pierre Fernier. He'd known "Frenchy" for years, but only recently had bankrolled him. "I spent no time in the joint. I'm there maybe an hour, two hours a week to kill a little time and kibitz the action. It's a hundred to one they'll raid Fernier. He knows everybody in the county. It's another long shot that they'll grab me. The captain busts the door, the first thing he says, 'Whatcha doing here, Buckley? I didn't know you had a piece of this place.'"

I understood without his saying it that my father believed that because the operation had been raided, my brother and I should know his relationship to Fernier. Neither his tone nor his manner suggested that he was seeking forgiveness or reassurance, but at some level my father regarded a run-in with the law as a miscalculation, a failure. His response was to compromise his own deep commitment to bearing all responsibility without explanation to his family. My father ended by letting me know he was going to take a shot at "straightening out the case," and he would let me know how it progressed.

Uncle Mac, oldest of the five Offit brothers of my father's generation, visited briefly, as if making a condolence call. A thin man with an eagle face and regal bearing, Mac, through his years as a business leader and participant in social and philanthropic activities, had grown accustomed to expressing himself in short bursts of generalization—"people always resent their benefactors but that doesn't mean we should do away with the Marshall Plan, the Truman Doctrine, or the UJA." Although a streetwise and reasonably sophisticated man, Mac believed, as did most of my father's family and business associates—that his brother was invulnerable to the law. It was obvious that the newspaper story had come as a shock to him and his tone, if not his words, resembled the wailings of an inarticulate though well-intentioned mourner. "You. Why you? Why our Buck? The police have better things to do with their time than arrest a man like you—a man who does so much for so many people, who is charitable, a wonderful family man. Who'd you ever hurt? You've done nothing but good. The papers make too much of it. It doesn't even deserve mention. Embarrass you, your wife, your boys. Let me tell you I've met them all, compared to you the best of them are second-rate hypocrites. You've led a decent life, an honorable life . . . "

My father listened with amusement for a while. Then, he stopped rocking—always a signal. When he spoke his rasp was deeply authoritative. It allowed no argument. "What're you talking about, Mac?" my father said to his brother. "You're talking, you don't know what you're talking about. I'm a bookmaker. I been one all my life. They got a knock on a joint. They kicked it in. Charity's got nothing to do with it. So they write it up in the *Sun*. So what. I'm gonna do what I have to do."

The trial was in the early fall. I returned to Baltimore every other week to attend reserve meetings and follow the progress of my father's case. His busy routine I remembered from my childhood no longer served as a distraction. My father, as he had said, was "out—o-u-t—out" of the gambling business. He was up each morning at eight, fixed breakfast for my mother—juice, coffee, and toast—and passed the morning reading the Baltimore *Sun*, every page, every line. He regarded the action days of his past— booking, cards, craps—as over. Only the case remained as a reminder of his once active and frequently perilous history.

My father adjusted to his new routine without complaint or boredom. In the afternoon he would take a long walk with the family terrier Raimey, who at the age of eight strained at the leash with a mite less ferocity. After being fed, Raimey would nap at his feet during the late afternoon. When the *Evening Sun* came at five, my father received it with the respect due a Shakespeare folio. He scanned the front page and then passed immediately to the sports section to track the athletes and columns of narrative with which he was already familiar from the early edition. When an *Evening Sun* story devoted a paragraph to his forthcoming trial, he seemed indifferent to the exclusion of his name. I asked him if this was an item he had "straightened out." He told me he knew nothing about the report.

As I sat with my father in the pale light of the enclosed porch of the Seville Apartments, we went from a discussion of the trial to talk about legalized gambling. "You take the average working stiff, he gets a shot at the books or lotteries, he's gonna drop a lot of paychecks better spent on groceries or clothes for his kids." He puffed on his cigarette before he said, "but there's no law I ever seen or heard of gonna stop people from gamblin'. Far as I can make out gamblin' is part of human nature."

We sat silently for a long while. I was accustomed to the quiet warmth of my father's company and knew that more often than not nothing more would be said unless I spoke first. I asked my father about his handling of the case. "How's it going in the county? Think you have a chance?"

A window was open and the fall chill permeated the room. It was close to dinnertime and I could smell simmering onions, roasting beef, garlic, and warm bread. "I got a lawyer with contacts in the valley," my father told me. "I'm giving him a good package. He's a former state's attorney and in with the judge."

My father spoke so matter-of-factly I had to think for a moment to realize that the situation he was describing involved tampering and bribery. Yet, I felt no fear—even the warmth of the room seemed as comforting as the kitchen smells. I wanted to know more.

"Does that mean the judge is in on it, too?" I asked. "He gets paid for letting you off?" Before my father could answer, I said, "You know, I may want to write about this some day, Dad. I think what you're doing, how you do it—" I

could not quite say the words, "bribe, fix"—
"tells us something important about how our
system works."

My father scowled, gently. "Important?" He
repeated, "nothin' important about me, Sid. I do
what I got to do," he said. "The county is gonna
get three convictions. They got Frenchy cold
and two of the guys at the phones. It wasn't
even my joint. I'm paying the nut for the whole
mess. Still—you never know. The judge is a
gentleman, he believes 'live and let live,' I'll walk
out of it. He takes my money and goes the other
way, I'll do time. They say it's only tough for the
first twenty-four hours." He stood suddenly,
and rubbed Raimey behind the ears. The terrier
made a small sound deep in her throat and followed my dad to the dining room. "Let's scarf a
little," my father said. "Tomorrow could be
bread and water."

Two days before the trial my father invited me
to come along with him on a drive downtown.
He was going to Tony's Barber Shop for a trim
and manicure and later in the morning had an

appointment at the Lord Baltimore Hotel with the captain of the county's vice squad. All of this seemed very routine and I deciphered not the slightest sign of anxiety or self-consciousness in my father.

The last time I'd been to Tony's was the day before my bar mitzvah. The visit to my father's barbershop had seemed as much a rite of passage as my reading of the ancient law. I recognized the proprietor, who was often referred to in the third person as Tough Tony. Tony had been a professional boxer before the days when Italian names became acceptable in the ring. He fought under the pseudonym Tom O'Neil and from time to time familiar customers would refer to him as Tommy or O'Neil. I found it confusing and unintelligible when I was thirteen, but at twenty-three it contributed to my feeling of affection and familiarity. Tony greeted me with a hug and clipped my jaw. "He looks pretty good, the old man, huh? They not going to get Papa so easy. You can bet on that."

My hair was unusually long and Tony took this as invitation. As he cut my hair I saw the reflection of my father in the mirror: He was talking to a bearded man in a winter overcoat and giving him money. Later, as Tony cut my father's hair, the manicurist and the shoeshine attendant got to work. Personal service and attention embarrassed me, and I was surprised that my father was so comfortable with these ministrations. They seemed comforting rituals to him, and in some way he regarded submitting to the amenities of the barbershop as an aspect of being a good sport, sharing the wealth.

A heavyset pug-faced man in a visored golf cap was particularly intent on talking to my father. He had been reading the *Telegraph* when we arrived, but he put the paper aside and stood close to Buckley, nodding with an expression that alternated between beaming admiration and barely controlled agony. After abundant tipping and reassurances, my father and I left Tony's and started walking towards the Lord Baltimore. The man in the visored cap followed us out the door. The first words I heard him speak were grim: "I don't know, Buckley. I just don't know if I can do time." My father's answer was direct but not impatient. "You got no choice, Bronc. You going to do a little time one way or the other. Least you know, the clock is running, you're making seventy-five a week with five c-notes waiting for you when you get out."

It was one of the few times I was witness to the dealings and persuasions that were part of my father's work. I knew Bronc must be one of the two men who were operating the phones at Pierre Fernier's the afternoon of the raid. In return for Bronc's guilty plea, my father was obviously paying a salary during the time he served in jail. I considered the dialogue intimidating and threatening. If Bronc elected to talk to the police about my father's role as a banker, it was likely that the danger would considerably increase. Much as I identified with my father, I couldn't help thinking of movie scenes where the felon who took the rap tried to shake down "Mr. Big."

We walked silently for a while. I fell in step with my father and avoided eye contact with Bronc, who ambled at our side shrugging his shoulders and flinching his eyes to indicate he was not entirely satisfied. My father turned suddenly and faced Bronc. Although Bronc was a head taller than my father and had the look of a man accustomed to violence, my father's voice was a deep guttural, definitive and challenging. "Let me tell you something, Bronc. I'm not at Frenchy's joint the day they kick it in, you got yourself a rap and nothing running for you. Understand that? Nothing. You'd do time and there'd not be two bits at the end of the walk. How many bets you seen me take at Frenchy's, Bronc? How many phones I answer?"

Bronc's expression indicated these were thoughts he hadn't previously contemplated. He shrugged. "You right, Big O," he said. "I got no knock against you. You're tops. Without you we all be out in the cold." Then, he said, "I never done time before. They tell me . . . "

Before he could finish my father cut him off. "They tell you? Who the hell are *they*? You got better sense than to listen to what the red board players tell ya, Bronc." My father stopped speaking as abruptly as he had interrupted. He punched the taller man lightly on the chest. His tone was soft, affectionately gentle now. "I seen you take worse shots from that Polack kid from Pennsylvania fifteen years ago at the Coliseum. You'll be all right, Bronc. Just mind yer own

business. Keep yer mouth shut and kill time."
My father's hand moved to his pocket. "You
know whatcha need, Bronc? A few days rest and
a new hat." He pulled several bills from his
pocket and without looking at the denominations handed them to Bronc. "Take a couple
days at that joint you usta train at near Anne-
runnel. Breathe a little fresh air, take some
walks. Clean yerself up. Ya look like a bum. You
never looked so bad, Bronc. Sure, you took a
knock. We all take our lumps. You make the
best of it. Buy yerself a new hat and keep going."

Bronc's expression changed subtly. He lifted
his head and momentarily seemed to swagger.
He took off his hat. "This ain't my hat, Buckley.
I don't even know what I'm doing with it." He
examined the bills in his wad. "Hey, you don't
owe me nothing, Big O. Come on, I'm not looking to shake you down."

"Forget it," my father said. "I'll deduct it from
yer salary."

Bronc turned to me. "That is some old man
you got there, kiddo. Don't you worry about
him. None of us gonna let anybody lay a hand
on Buckley. Nosirree bah."

We continued on our way past the shops of downtown Baltimore, traversing the Block, a stretch of Baltimore Street that housed night-clubs, strip bars, and souvenir shops specializing in photographs of naked women and out-of-date publications—*Police Gazette, Eye, See*—that offered various views of the unclad or horrific. My father walked with his felt hat pulled low over his eyes, acknowledging occasional greet-ings with a nod or hand to the visor but allowing no conversation. I knew that the owners of sev-eral of the more notorious spots on the block were former associates of my dad. During my childhood, Sammy Miller, who later owned the Oasis, a club known for its lascivious entertain-ment and sexy bar-girls, visited our house to check the week's accounts with Buckley. A wry man with a pixie smile and affection for the opera, Sammy always had a word for my mother. I thought about the former book-maker—strip-joint proprietor—reflecting on the anomalies of Strauss and Hofmannsthal's *Ariadne auf Naxos.*

I was wondering about the moral paradoxes of my own life. Flush with the confidence engendered by my college and Army experience, it occurred to me to advise my dad. It was one thing to break the gaming laws of the state of Maryland, another to tamper with the rigid codes of the legal system. Yet I knew he considered it his responsibility to deal with his case without consideration for other people's rules or laws. I wasn't sure if he wasn't in for even more trouble because of his self-defined morality.

When we got to the hotel, my father told me to wait outside while he met with the vice-squad captain. "Take a walk around the block. I'll pick you up on the late shift." I started to the corner, but got no farther than that. I wasn't acquainted with the officer my dad was meeting; he wouldn't recognize me. I decided to wait outside the hotel entrance. The nearness to my father felt safer. Several minutes after my father left me, a tall, lean man wearing a grey suit and no topcoat double-parked and with long, loping strides entered the Lord Baltimore. He had the wholesome good looks of Jimmy Stewart, but I knew the moment he glanced up and down the block that he was the police officer with whom my father had "done business."

◆

*   *   *

The morning of the trial my father was up early
and made breakfast for my mother. She had
maintained a characteristic calm and confidence through the long weeks between the raid
and the trial. Mother was reading Montaigne's
essays, having started on the first volume during
my junior year at the Hopkins. She read slowly
but frequently quoted passages to me. The
French essayist was concerned with pain and
death in his first volume. Then he moved on to
considerations of knowledge and the accept-
ance of life. With Montaigne as scripture, my
mother exhausted her pessimism and came to
terms with my father's ordeal. *"Toutes actions,
hors les bornes ordinaires sont sujettes a sinistres
interpretations,"* she tried in her self-taught
French. The translation—"all unusual actions
are liable to sinister interpretations," seemed to
me soothing. My father hugged my mother
before my brother, he, and I set out for the
court in Towson. He kissed her on both cheeks
and said, "Well, Libby, my old man always told
me I should've been a tailor."

Seated in the cold, grey courthouse—high ceiling, marble busts, nineteenth-century portraits of deceased magistrates—it was painful to realize we were on the other side of the law. The conservatively dressed, square-jawed former state's attorney who represented my father and all the accused seemed to want to have no more to do with any of us than was absolutely necessary. The trial proceeded as if choreographed by an impatient stage director. The county presented its case with three witnesses. Captain Burke of the vice-squad, whom I recognized as the man my father had met at the hotel, spoke with an earnest, no-nonsense voice that drawled just enough to suggest a connection with the southern traditions of western Maryland. If you believed in the hero of *Mr. Smith Goes to Washington,* you had to trust every word he said. The significant part of his testimony was that he identified only three of the defendants as working on the phones at the time of the raid. There were no defense witnesses. After the prosecution presented its case, Fernier, Bronc, and the other defendant—a long-haired, middle-aged gentleman in a three-piece suit—pleaded guilty. The case against my father was declared a "stet." It was the first and only time I had heard that familiar editing term used in a court of law. To this day I'm not certain of its application, but my father walked out of the courthouse with us—a free man.

But I wasn't. When I returned to New York to resume writing, I abandoned the novel I'd started about life at a military school. I wanted to write a novel about my father. Bookmakers and gamblers in fiction always appeared as caricatures derived from Damon Runyon, or dark, sinister, potentially violent figures as portrayed in the movies by George Raft or Edward G. Robinson. I saw my father as noble, with an indigenous American quality of self-reliance, a man who lived by his own code. I wanted to write about him and yet it seemed impossible without discussing the way he dealt with the justice system. I couldn't make up a story that would be convincingly sympathetic to the fix, to bribery, to the corruption of the law.

I considered casting my father in a more formidable role—the head of a crime family. But that was a world with which I wasn't familiar and an element of society for which I discovered my father had neither affinity nor awe.

When I visited a week after the trial my father was mellow and reflective. I asked him about his relationship to organized crime. "They tried to move in on Buzz and me in the thirties. A couple of them would-be wiseguys from Boston told us they wanted to speak to us. If I'm not mistaken, you was there that morning. Make a long story short—they come around and Buzz had the dogs out. That big retriever—what's his name?"

"*Dauber*," I tried.

"Nah. *Dauber* won the Preakness in 'thirty-eight. Musta been before that." He smoked and rocked, thinking intensely. "Peters was up. Arcaro had his first Derby winner—*Lawrin*—the same year. Couldn't a'been 'thirty-eight. Anyway, with the dogs scratchin', Buzz says, 'Let's give them hyenas something to think about.' Soon as their car pulls up he's waiting with a half-cocked shotgun."

My father seemed to consider that the end of

the story and I had to cajole him to provide other details. The only exchange of dialogue he remembered was the colonialists from Boston suggesting that for a small charge they would provide protection for Buzz and him. Buzz's answer, my father recalled, was succinct. "Gentlemen, the only people you can protect us from is yourselves." My father's contempt for what I later recognized as the Mafia or the Mob was so absolute I could never write or even read about them without loathing.

Another time he told me about an encounter with Al Capone in Hot Springs in the twenties. "I run into the bum coming down the main drag. He's got five, six of them tough guys from Chicago all over him. Bodyguards. He gives me the high sign. He's got a little action, wants me to book to him. I say, 'No thank you, Mr. Capone. I'm down here fer vacation. No time for business.' He says, 'No time?' Gives me that Guinea smile. I just tell him again, 'No time.' I keep walkin'. A day later I'm talkin' a little this and that with Always Al Friedman who's got a joint near the Arlington. Always Al tells me he's booked to the bum. I tell Always Al, you book to Capone, you might as well throw yer money down the crapper. Capone wins, he wants to be paid. He loses, I'll bet you a new hat, you'll never see a dime."

Again, I had to encourage my father to complete the story. He seemed to regard it as obvious that the Hot Springs bookie's experience with Al Capone would only end one way. "Next winter Lily and me are down for the baths, I get a note from Always Al waiting for me at the Arlington. He's got a seven-and-one-half Stetson waiting for me. I tell him, 'No thanks, Al. But you make a move to pay off. Pretty good at that. Yer more a gentleman than that tough guy Capone.' I got no respect for him, none at all." Then my father said, "I wear a seven-and-one-eighth."

CHAPTER XIII

Glass Eye and Cane

◆ *Hagerstown 1953* ◆

A telephone call in the night. Avi and I are visiting Baltimore. My mother, Avi, Benson, and I have returned from dinner at Miller Brothers. We're deep in conversation when the phone rings. I pick it up. The voice at the other end—somber and urgent—identifies himself as a police officer. He wants to know if I'm a relative of Buckley Offit. When he hears I'm his son, he says, "Your father has been in an automobile accident. It would be best if you came to Hagerstown Hospital as soon as possible." He seems sympathetic but unwilling to spell out details. Yes, my father is still alive, but unconscious. The injury appears serious.

The family Buick is low on gas. It's past mid-

◆

night and the stations in downtown Baltimore are closed. Benson drives. Avi sits at his side, reading the map. My mother and I are in the back seat. Mother sets the emotional tone. She is neither hysterical nor pessimistic. "Buck will be all right," she repeats. "I know my Buckley will be all right." She recites the reassuring clichés by which my father lives. "Take one thing at a time. Don't make problems."

I can't control my imagination. I'm convinced my father is dead. I suspect the policeman held back the bad news as a courtesy. He will not tell us my father has been killed until he faces us in person.

The quest for gas diverts us and once we make a wrong turn but we get to Hagerstown at dawn. An attendant at the hospital tells us our father was brought in bleeding and unconscious. It's important to minimize all contact or movement. They will not wipe up the blood or change his clothes until the brain damage is assessed. We're allowed a brief visit. The left side of my father's face is crushed and disfigured. There's a long red and mucousy streak where the eye should be. We are all in tears now.

◆

A doctor tells us that my father has lost his left eye, which was destroyed by the window adjuster of the backseat, where he was sitting at the time of the accident. We aren't concerned with identifying the driver or the circumstances of the accident, but concentrate on the medical problems. My mother suggests we call Uncle Julius, my father's brother who is active in philanthropy and is on the board of the Sinai Hospital in Baltimore. There's no diagnosis of the condition of the right eye. We call Dr. Herman Krieger Goldberg, an ophthalmologist for whom we know our father has affection. Dr. Goldberg will leave for Hagerstown immediately. Uncle Julius speaks to the chief of brain surgery at Sinai. He, too, will come to Hagerstown. I'm concerned that we have offended the sensitivities of the local staff. Benson, who is usually more considerate of others' feelings than I am, cannot accept what he regards as an exaggerated concern for protocol at a time like this. He wants to be by my father's side—available should he wake, attentive and protective. I'm not comfortable with this vigilance and am relieved when the reigning physician suggests we take a walk, have breakfast, try to unwind.

A bright fall Sunday. My mother and Avi retire to the hospital cafeteria for coffee. I remain with Benson whom I've never seen so agitated. I'm trying to be like my father, toughing it out. I'm surprised by my own reactions because I don't find this difficult. My brother and I are sitting on a bench looking out over the slope of a grassy knoll down to the hospital parking lot where the morning shift is arriving, nurses in white shoes, white uniforms, white caps. Benson doesn't want to speak or move. I decide he deserves indulgence, so I absorb myself speculating about the accident. I remember that my father visits Hagerstown for Saturday craps and card games. He had given up bookmaking after the Kefauver Committee's investigations of crime led to the passage of a federal law requiring a stamp for all professional gamblers. My father thinks that to apply for the stamp would be an invitation for the local authorities to arrest him. But he will not violate a federal statute. "It's tough enough fixing the locals," he says. "I'm not taking on the feds."

So his partner Buzz has arranged this weekly venture with the gentry in the neighborhood. "It's a night's work," says my dad. "And no chance anybody is gonna bust the joint." Buzz handles the dice. My dad deals the poker hands. They're back to where they were forty years ago—before the wagers with the aristocrats of thoroughbred racing. My father considers the Kefauver hearings a sham. "What they come up with—Frank Costello's hands and a fifty buck sticker that won't mean nothing to the mob. All they done is put me out of business."

I suggest a cup of coffee and Benson wearily rises. He's taller than I, broader of shoulder, a handsome young man with almond eyes, olive skin, and a warm cocky smile. We don't look alike and I see no resemblance in Benson to either parent. Yet he has inherited the good looks of the Offits and is by family consensus my father's son. I have the dark circles and full lips of my mother, the disproportionately muscular thighs and legs of her athletic brothers. I know I'm my mother's son. But I listen and hear, admire and believe and wish to be shaped by my father's courage, calm pragmatism, and delight in life. I'm conscious of this as I walk with my brother and try to understand the great difference in our confrontation with fear and death.

I touch his shoulder. He pats my hand, but clearly wishes no contact. In the cafeteria he has coffee with cream and sugar. I satisfy my fantasy of the ploughman's breakfast.

Our mother and my wife have left the cafeteria. We know they're waiting in the hospital lobby. But I eat the fried eggs, finish all the potatoes and bacon, and wipe up the yolks with toast. When I'm done, my brother says, "How could you eat! I don't understand you, Sid. Is that all you can think about, your own appetite?" Benson has quit after one sip of his coffee. My brother is no histrionic; this is no act. Though it occurs to me briefly, I know he isn't competitively mourning. He has the vulnerability of the little boy who never quite grows up. I say, "I'm sorry, Benly. To tell you the truth I could even go for a Danish." A poor try at humor but I'm full of appetite, maybe too hungry.

In the lobby we discover the tribe of Offits

has descended like the Maccabees joining Judas against the Syrians of Antiochus. All five brothers—Mac, Sam, Julius, Mike, and Eddie—are there, and so is sister Ida. They have notified each other by phone, made travel arrangements in minutes, and driven the seventy-five miles on route 40 to rally for their brother. Dr. Goldberg has arrived. Julius has also delivered the head of the department of brain surgery at Sinai. "An excellent man. I don't have to tell you we want the best, the very best for your dad."

Mike, who shared a bed with my father through the early years of their impoverished childhood, and Mac, the elder, and quiet Sam, and irrepressible Eddie gather around me. I hold court, reporting all the physicians have told me. As I mention that my father has lost an eye, I hear Eddie say, "What can I do to help? Anything. I'd do anything for Buckley. I'll give blood. Let me give my blood." He's the youngest of the Offit sons and always in a state of siege, if not at war, with all his brothers except my dad. Ida sits with my mother and I know I must try to protect my mother from the possessiveness of my father's sister, from her critical attitude towards mother's domestic management. By mother's side sits my wife Avi—pale and elegant. Strands of her long hair are loose from her chignon and the seam of one stocking is slightly crooked, but Avi sits erect, her dancer's body poised, a supportive presence for my mother.

"The next twenty-four hours are crucial," I hear myself repeat the doctor's words. "As soon as Dad comes out of the coma—if he does— they'll be able to determine if he's suffered a concussion or real brain damage." Benson cannot repeat these words, whose implications are too grim for him to bear. I'm not surprised when he tells me, "What do we need all the uncles for? Nobody loves Dad the way we do. No one cares as much as we do."

I've been performing with my father's injuries as a script. I've been observing, too, and unlike my brother I'm moved by this show of family support. I see my father, the ultimate gambler and prince of the streets, wounded on a highway as he returns from battle. "I got no regrets. . . .

I do what I want. . . . Nobody to blame but myself. Self-pity stinks." If this is his end I must respond in his own terms.

The brain surgeon from Sinai needs my mother's permission to take my father by ambulance to Baltimore. Should he need an operation there are better facilities there, but the trip is a risk. The bookmaker's wife has no hesitation responding to the odds. The surgeon will travel in the ambulance with him. Benson wants to join him. As I sit in the car beside my wife, I think of my father carried as Hector, the son of Priam, from the gates of Troy. The Offit caravan departs Hagerstown, leaving behind my father's eye.

A little more than forty-eight hours after Buzz King's four-door Cadillac, in which my father was a passenger, entered route 40 south from Hagerstown and was struck by a southbound truck, my father awakens. He's in a hospital room at Sinai; the brain surgeon and my brother are by his side. He says, "What's gone on here?" But he identifies his son and the month and, with a little prodding, the day of the year. Brain damage is unlikely.

◆

"We'll tell him about the lost eye as soon as he asks but no later than this evening," Dr. Goldberg tells us. Benson is disconcerted by what he considers the physician's presumption. "We'd like to think about that," my brother says. "Our father is a great man—he deserves more than a routine announcement that he has only one eye." Dr. Goldberg, swarthy, dark-eyed, with the looks of John Garfield and the manner of Claude Rains, is not insulted. "Discuss it with your mother, of course," he says. "But don't underrate your dad. I'm sure Buck will adjust easily."

Benson says, "I never underrate my father."

Later, Benson tells me he's concerned for our father's feelings. "Close one eye," my brother directs me. "The world feels different with one eye. You have to think if the other eye is injured, you're blind." My brother tries to suffer my father's accident empathetically. I have already come to terms with my father's loss. I have distanced myself from imagining and contemplating life with one eye. I remember my father saying: "Life don't owe me nothing." I believe him.

◆

It's settled in less than two minutes. Dr. Goldberg tells my father about the injury and Benson, my mother, and I are invited into his room. A large patch covers my father's left eye. The doctor has told him he'll need some reconstructive surgery for the cheek. The right eye is fine, undamaged by the accident.

My father smiles when we enter the room. "I won another long shot," he says. "I don't remember nothing from the accident except some guy near me saying, 'This one is bleeding like a pig. He's got no chance.' Then I went out."

Benson comes to his side. His eyes fill with tears. "You'll be able to read with one eye, Dad, and drive a car. If you need me, I'll drive for you." I believe my father is as unaffected as a person can be under the circumstances. "I'm still here," he says. "I got one good blinker. They'll put in one of them glass pieces, I'll still pick winners."

From time to time during the next few years I close my left eye and read or walk or survey a meadow or the sky. I do this briefly and then close both eyes. I open them quickly. My father continues to drive a car for three more decades.

After numerous dents and cacophonies of horns, he finally surrenders his license in 1983. True to his word, my brother drives him to the grocer, the doctor, the barber, and, of course, to his son and daughter-in-law's house where my parents have dinner every Friday night. I don't recall my father ever mentioning that he has one eye. When I ask him how he's able to adjust so quickly and without complaint, he says, "What's the good talking about it, you can't buy or make another eye. I got a good break, at that."

I feel like the little boy at the window, watching my father battling the hoods. I'm unable to help him and yet I feel he needs no help. His vision with one eye is no less clear than his perception of the world with two—relentlessly realistic, devoid of self-pity, unsentimental but at the same time grateful to the historical chance that has given him what he considers a winning ticket.

Only Heaven Can
Tell—1992

*Mid-August, several weeks before his ninety-sixth
birthday, my father was taken to Sinai Hospital to
treat his transient ischemic attacks. Rosie, the
housekeeper-companion who stayed with him
during the day, had observed him fading out, los-
ing consciousness, and she had wisely called an
ambulance. He was sitting up in bed the afternoon I came to visit. It was a warm summer day.
My father's face—collapsed around the missing
left eye and covered by several days' growth of
beard—was nonetheless animated when he
greeted me. "I dunno what they got me in here
for," he said. "What they gonna do fer me? Then
again I gotta thank 'em for giving it a shot." We
talked about his grandchildren—Ken, Mike,*

Andy, Meg, and Tom. *He followed each of their careers and expressed satisfaction without overstated pride. I tried to get him going on Meg's job at the White House (Benson and Suzie's daughter had won a presidential internship) but all he would say is, "They all doing okay—that doctor son of yers trying to find a way to beat cancer. Andy and Mike bangin' heads with the money guys. Tom hittin' the books." He shrugged and smiled. We talked about his great-grandchildren—Anna, Caroline, and Tristan, and he said, "Lily sure got a kick outta them." Then he said, "What's the ussa talkin'? What's done is done."*

He turned away from me and stared at the blank TV monitor. We were silent for a while. I studied my father's aged, almost skeletal silhouette. After a long silence I asked, "What're you thinking, Dad?"

"This and that . . . "

"Do you remember past moments, particular experiences?"

His voice was so soft I could barely hear him. "I think about Lily . . . about things we done together . . . "

I said, "Well, Dad, you may be seeing her

◆

again. Who knows? I'm not trying to sell you religion, but a lot of people do believe there's some kind of afterlife, a place where souls meet."

My father turned toward me with an expression that indicated surprise. "Who tole you about that? What you gettin' at, Sid?"

"I'm not saying there is or there isn't, but a lot of people are convinced there's more to life than just what goes on earth."

"Anybody ever come back and told you about that?" my father asked. He turned away from me and back to the blank TV screen. "This is it, Sid," he said. "I got no regrets. I come in a long shot. My number's up, it's up."

Two days later I was back in New York and my father had returned from the hospital. I had forgotten his handicapping the Travers until I read the results in the paper. On the twenty-second of August at Saratoga Springs Thunder Rumble outran Devil His Due and Dance Floor; he paid seven to one. If I'd parlayed my father's theoretical winnings of $2,590, we'd have more than $18,000. It was beginning to be more than a little complicated pretending to book to my old man.

◆

CHAPTER XIV

The Last Parlay

Three days before my mother died, Avi and I visited her at the Johns Hopkins Hospital. Her room overlooked the rear of the three-story building and the familiar dome fronting on Broadway. This is the neighborhood where my grandmother—my mother's mother—had the small grocery catering to local residents and medical students. On the white stone steps of adjacent buildings that billeted the house staff, my mother has told me she often passed summer evenings in the company of interns and residents, whom she remembered as "southern gentlemen, courtly, studious, and shy." It's several days after the cardiologist has tested her heart and reported that the damage to the artery leading to the rear of her heart is so diffuse there is no possibility of corrective surgery.

My mother isn't connected to respirators or IVs, but she's weak and the doctors have told us that, given the damage to her heart, it's miraculous that she continues to live. The nurses speak admiringly of her spirit. "Your mother is quite a fighter. That is one tough lady."

On an impulse I buy a box of Fanny Farmer assorted chocolates in the hospital gift shop. Avi gets a small flowered plant. Mother is sleeping when we arrive at her room. Her face is so shrunken, her hands so lined and blue, only the gentle movement of her chest tells me she's alive. As soon as she wakes up and is aware there are visitors in her room, she reaches for her glasses. She speaks Avi's name first. Even after nearly forty years, I am pleased that my mother's response to my wife's presence is so much like my own. My mother is mildly alarmed. "Why are you here?" she asks. "Am I dying?" Before we can answer, she says, "I know I'm dying." I hold her hand. Avi strokes the old white head.

I give her the box of candy. It's more a nostalgic gesture than a useful gift. I remind my mother of the boxes of Whitman's chocolates Benson and I bought forty, fifty years ago as last-minute gifts for her birthday or Mother's Day. She quietly guided us to more enduring symbols—Doulton dogs, antiques from Sara Shiller's, etchings and prints from Bachrach's. I mention her lessons in taste and hope she will find solace in the familiar names. My mother nods. Her lips tremble.

Avi and I sit by her bed as she samples the assorted chocolates. It's a ritual of my childhood, watching my mother test pieces of chocolate for the fillings she prefers. Why do I remember that she always passes up the candied cherries? I recall, too, that the caramels are usually square and there's frequently a small almond on top of the shredded coconut. My mother bites, examines, discards a jellied filling. She tries again and seems satisfied with a peppermint. Avi and I exchange glances; we are both amused and encouraged.

"Take the box away," my mother says suddenly. "I've eaten enough. Mustn't upset my stomach." Then, she turns to Avi and clutches her hand. "I don't want to die," she says. "Don't let me die."

I've heard these words from my mother before and I try not to be affected by them. But because she's asking for a miracle from my wife, I feel a need to protect Avi from the need to lie and fail. I say, "Don't talk like that, Ma. You're in great shape. You just knocked off half a dozen chocolates, you're a long way from gone." I'm imitating the rhetoric of my father; I hear my voice mimicking him. Avi kisses my mother's forehead. She says, "My, isn't this a lovely room?"

My mother nods agreement. She is sleeping when we leave.

On Monday morning, the first day of April, my brother calls at 8:40 to tell me, "Mom died last night, Sid." At her request there is no funeral, just a brief service at the graveside. Ken and his wife Emily, Mike and his wife Dara have come from New York to join our family and friends on the greening Maryland hillside drenched in spring sun. Cantor Saul Hammerman chants the ancient Kaddish, and we repeat, "Yisgadal v'yiskadash sh'me rabbo, b'olmo d'hoo oosid l'itchad' to ul'achayo-oh . . . " The prayers are filled with praise of God. Nothing in the recitation reminds me of my mother. My father sits, hunched, a small and wizened head beneath the Borsalino hat that is a remnant of the days when he banked his money in shoeboxes and tipped the brims of boaters and fedoras to the lords of the track. Uncle Eddie and Aunt Ida, the last of their generation of the Offits in Baltimore, flank my dad. I know my mother is in the oak coffin, sealed forever from a touch, a word, a smile. I feel sadness but no overwhelming grief. My mind wanders . . . I wonder if with the death of my mother I have lost my last link to faith. Who will remind me now of the richness of the Jewish tradition and bond me to it with memories of a grandfather who was a *Kohan?*

I bring back an image of my mother from an old photograph: hand to the crown of a broad-brimmed hat, a flowered summer dress, small looped earrings, strapped pumps, as she walks with my brother and me along Atlantic City's boardwalk. It's not the physical image of my mother that is too deep for tears but the memory of her voice reading.

My mind is groggy with the exhaustion of grief as I silently commemorate the memory of my mother, the reader. She often spoke of devotion to her father, a Hebrew scholar. I know she believed in the rituals and teachings of our people, but I cannot remember a line, a thought my mother quoted to me from the abundance of Jewish theology she so admired. It may be a failing or a romantic pretension, but it is Stevenson I recall my mother reciting ("And all around I heard you pass/Like ladies' skirts across the grass. . . .") and Browning ("The year's at the spring, the day's at the morn . . .") and most resonant of all, the words of Montaigne. She read slowly, thoughtfully, three volumes. During my late adolescence and college years she would spring upon me suddenly with an idea, a rumination of the French essayist (attempted in her tentative effort at self-taught French): *"Je veux . . . que le morte me trouve plantant mes choux, mais nonchalant d'elle, et encore plus de mon jardin imparfait."* "Planting cabbages when

I die but too exhausted from life to care anymore," she paraphrases, smacks her lips, and points a finger at me as if we are engaged in debate. "Planting cabbages means at least his body is functioning. That's better than dying paralyzed in bed. Good for Montaigne! Good for me!"

I'm thinking, too, that my mother would have appreciated the simple dignity of her graveside rites. When the prayers are done, Benson comes forward to deliver the eulogy. He's wearing a blue blazer and grey slacks, a blue shirt and dark rep tie. His shoulders are now permanently rounded. I'm observing these details as I hear his eloquent sketch of our mother's life. Benson's oratorical devices are instinctive and genuine, but I find myself analyzing them. I notice that he creates his best effects when he repeats a name and simultaneously registers a feeling that seems to leave him unable to find the next word. "And Rosie . . . how can I say enough about Rosie . . . Rosie . . . Always there as nurse, friend . . . family." There are the sounds of sobbing. My brother turns at last to an impression of our parents' relationship:

"Why was it Mama lived through nine decades? How was she able to survive her three brothers, her two sisters? When I asked Mom, she never hesitated. Her answer was one word. One word . . . 'Bucky. My Bucky.'" The testimony is true and sincerely spoken. I put aside my own intrusive memories of Henry MacKenzie's eighteenth-century novel, *The Man of Feeling*. Do I remember correctly? Did he weep himself to death?

My brother ends with the last scene between my mother and father. It was the Sunday night before she died and Benson and his daughter Meg were visiting the hospital. Dad had fallen again that afternoon, but later in the day he insisted he wanted to visit his wife.

"Just before we left Mom, she turned toward the door and called to us," Benson recalls. "She wanted to speak to Dad. Meg and I were standing at the door and Dad was at her bedside when we heard her say, 'You know I love you, Buck. I've always loved you, Bucky. I always will.'" My brother describes how my father touched his hand to my mother's head and kissed her good-bye. "Then Dad said, 'I love you

twice as much, Lily.' Sixty-three years together,"
Benson reminds us. "I can't think of a better
ending."

I'm moved and proud of this classic saluta-
tion to marriage, family, life. But my eyes wan-
der to observe the effects of my brother's words
on my daughters-in-law. I'm concerned that
Emily and Dara hear and care and remember
so they can share our family history with my
parents' great-grandchildren. Everywhere I look,
eyes are filled with tears. Avi huddles close and
puts her arm around my shoulders. I am sixty-
two years old, I remind myself again, I'm experi-
encing the death of my mother who was so close
to me I sometimes felt myself a spiritual clone.
It's my mother's funeral, and I—the champion
crybaby of them all—have not shed a tear.

Cantor Hammerman chants the melodious
farewell that returns my mother to the mysteries of time and ends that are beginnings. I move
to my father's side. I walk with him to the car
that is to take us to my brother's house, where
we will sit shiva. My father's white and ancient

head is contorted by grief. He holds his glass eye in a handkerchief and sobs. It's the first time in my life I have seen him cry. Through the rattle of his sobs I hear him say, "The picnic is over. All over, Lily. No more ice cream. I lost my last parlay."

I'm the little boy who once stood helplessly by the window and never forgave himself for being unable to come to his father's aid. I put my arm around his shoulder and cry, too.

Happy Birthday— 1992

The last time I saw my dad was the anniversary of his ninety-sixth birthday. I came down to Baltimore for a celebration with Uncle Eddie and Benson. We had planned a late lunch at Marconi's, but it was my father's first outing after his hospital visit and he said he preferred "a joint in the neighborhood." After a lunch of club sandwiches and beer, my father said he'd like some dessert. The club sandwich featuring a premium slice of ham hadn't been a big hit with him, so he suggested, "We give this place the duck and go to an ice cream joint."

His appetite was fine, but his heart condition now required round-the-clock nursing, and when I sat with him later that afternoon he seemed tired *and worried. My father had never asked for nor seemed to require support or reassurance and even now, when the doctor told my brother our father could die at any moment, I knew he would find it difficult to ask for help.* I said, "What's on your mind, Pop? You were always in there for me when I needed a lift, you gotta let me do the same for you."

His voice came out with the old familiar growl: "I dunno what I need all this nursin' fer. Must be costin' Benson a big me-ow."

"Don't even think about it, Dad," I said. "Avi and I are doing fine. We can pick up the tab and it won't come close to what we owe you."

"You owe me?" my father said. "You owe me nothin'."

"How about all those winners you gave me— Strike the Gold, Thunder Rumble *in the Jim Dandy and the Travers. We started with ten bucks and now you have eighteen thousand bucks in the pot. What d'you want me to do with it?"*

"Yeah," my father said with the wry smile that crossed his face when he knew someone was trying to put something over on him. "You got as much chance bettin' that kind of money as I got writin' a book." Then he said, "It don't make no difference, Sid. You do what you gotta do. That's all you can ask of yerself in this world."

I gave it a last try. "Don't worry about the nursing bills, Dad. What Medicare doesn't cover, Avi and I will be happy to pay. And I'm right in there for Benson, just the way you and Mom were for us."

"I know you ain't gonna ever let yer kid brother down, Sid," he said. "That's good enough fer me."

I thought he was dozing as I started from the room, but then I heard my father rasp, "See what price November Snow is in the Ruffin or a filly name of Versatile Treaty—but don't make a habit of it."

Before I left Baltimore I asked my brother if Dad still read the newspapers or watched races. "He may," was Benson's answer, "but I'm not aware of it."

Our father died in his sleep October 7, 1992. After my brother and I visited the Sol Levinson funeral home to pick the casket, I wrote an obituary intended for the Baltimore *Sun*. When I called, the editor said he didn't remember ever publishing an obituary that acknowledged a person's career as a bookmaker. He checked but found no mention of Buckley Offit in the paper's files. I appreciated the agreement to run the piece on the day of the funeral. It seemed to me my father's career should be acknowledged by the newspaper he had sold eighty years ago and the city he had lived in all his life.

His brother and sister didn't agree. Uncle Eddie said, "Bucky always tried to keep his name out of the papers." Aunt Ida who was ninety-two and not always aware of the nuances of a conversation told me, "You can't write in a newspaper that Buck was a bookie. It's against the law." Benson said it didn't make any difference to him one way or the other, it was up to me.

My nephew Tom, a graduate student in anthropology, wanted to know to whom the obituary was addressed. "Our family doesn't have to read about Gramps in the newspaper to know the kind of man he was." He convinced me to kill the piece when he asked, "What do you think Gramps would say?"

* * *

November Snow *was scratched but* Versailles Treaty *won the Ruffian. I didn't bet on him. Like my father said, I never got in the habit. My brother attended to the details of the funeral. With the exception of the Hamilton watch we'd bought for him for his seventy-fifth birthday and a ten thousand dollar no-interest bearing life insurance policy paid in full thirty-five years ago, my father left no estate. Uncle Eddie got the watch and I signed my share of the insurance over to Benson to help pay the nursing bills. I tried to give my brother a check for his share of Dad's last bet, but Benson knew right away I hadn't won it from OTB. We wondered why our dad had done his last handicapping with me and not Benson. But it didn't make any difference. One way or the other we'd share the same pot. Our dad knew that. He and my mother had prepared us a long time ago.*

◆